Tuning to the Spiritual Frequencies

"Everyone thoroughly enjoyed and acknowledged the vast knowledge gained at your Tuning to the Spiritual Frequencies workshop."

Jean Sabina
The Center of Human Growth
Vancouver, Canada

"Superbly done. I will be happy to sell Tuning to the Spiritual Frequencies at my seminars."

Donna Atkinson
New Vistas Reno, Nevada

"The stars are born out of whirling interstellar gases that heat up and light up. They radiate starlight for a billion years, then burn out. The gases disburse through the endless heavens eventually becoming part of the substance forming a new star across the galaxy.

"Birth, life, death and rebirth is the never-ending cycle of creation. From breath to breath, from heartbeat to heartbeat, we are a living creative process interconnected with every other creative process following archetypal geometric patterns."

From Chapter 14: The Science of Creativity

Tuning to the Spiritual Frequencies

By
Greg Nielsen
Conscious Books
Reno, Nevada

Tuning to the Spiritual Frequencies
by Greg Nielsen
CONSCIOUS BOOKS Reno, Nevada USA 800/322-9943

CONSCIOUS BOOKS 316 California Ave., Suite 210
Reno, Nevada 89509 USA
800/322-9943
greg.nielsen@charter.net

First Quality Paperback Edition 1990

10 9 8 7 6 5 4 3 2

Library of Congress Catalog Card Number: 89-091602

ISBN 0-9619917-1-2

Printed and Bound in The United States of America

Cover painting by visionary artist JOANNE DOSE

Cover design and prepress by WHITESAGE STUDIOS
Virginia City, Nevada.
whitsage@gbis.com

Dedication

To my teachers who took time to give me one-on-one guidance:

The Laguna Beach Carpenter
Agatha Verstoep
Francois Nesbitte
Isidore Friedman
Jane Mounts

Acknowledgements

The preparation of this book required the assistance of others for whom I am deeply grateful. Thank you,

Joanie Ward, for letting me use your computer, 1st printing.
Tracy Panzarella, for letting me use your computer, 2nd printing.
Mom, for entering the book in the computer.
Debra Sheehan, for your line drawings and editing.
Linda Knutesen, for your editing, 2nd printing.
Joanne, for your inspiring cover art.
Bob Bosler, for your creative text, 1st printing.
Paul Cirac, for your creative text, 2nd printing.

Table of Contents

Introduction

This book is a book about wisdom. Knowing what to do and doing it is wisdom. When you act wisely you shine a light. You are changed;the world is changed. Where there was chaos, confusion and darkness comes order, clarity and light.

This book is for those of you who are aware of life in a totally different way. Blind faith, ignorance and unconsciousness are no longer acceptable. You want to know; you need to know.

In the spring of 1969 I lay in a hospital bed dying of a rare blood disease. Deep within my soul stirred a feeling, the feeling that I had a choice to live or to die.

I thought if I decided to live I must find purpose in living otherwise why live? Obviously, I decided to live and found purpose in living.

It is wisdom to choose to live, to find your purpose for living and then live out your purpose.

Once you choose to live, to be alive, to be conscious, to leave old habits and beliefs behind, you enter an exciting, exhilerating phase. Your thirst for knowledge is quenchless. You want to know everything.

You begin to read, study, take classes, workshops and seminars. Your mind is filled with new knowledge, new possibilities.

If you persist in your learning, a new world opens to you. You know more. You're more aware. You are more sensitive. You experience new feelings of wonder, awe, beauty, peace, love, etc.

But along with these positive feelings your sensitivity makes you more aware of negative feelings as well. This is a critical time on the path because the question arises: How do you live in the world and handle the negative energies while maintaining your Tuning to the Spiritual Frequencies?

The path of wisdom is to choose to live everyday life with all its moil and turmoil yet maintain your Spiritual Tuning.

The purpose of this book is to assist you in living your life to the fullest, accepting and handling difficult life problems and transmuting negative energies into the light.

To me there is a Science of Living. When you are aware of the forces in any situation both in yourself and in the world you have choices. You can measure the wisdom of each choice, make your choice and then act consciously with measured energies.

As a result you act scientifically, wisely.

I have complimented the main text of this book with Light Waves, new age poems which inspire, guide, remind and instruct. I use the word Noetic several times in the poems and offer a brief explanation of its meaning.

The noetic consciousness is a state of clear seeing and knowing. If you place great value on awareness and practice it diligently you will eventually work your way into persistent and consistent noetic consciousness.

I urge you to read this book and see clearly what it is saying. But more importantly I urge you to test the practical ways presented and see what happens.

Remember: Knowing the way is not going the way.

Love, Light, Wisdom,

Greg Nielsen, May 1989

Chapter 1

The Divine Presence

Divine Presence is Cosmic Energy

The universe is permeated by a Divine Presence. Divine Presence is Cosmic Energy. Cosmic Energy interpenetrates everything in the universe.

Cosmic Energy is the substance of the universe, of our galaxy, solar system and planet. Whatever you look at is the visible condensation of cosmic energy.

Everything you see is sustained and maintained by cosmic energy. No thing ever dies. In reality, the cosmic energy flows in a different direction.

Your mind, body, soul and spirit are sustained and maintained by cosmic energy. When your time comes to make a transition from this world to the next, the cosmic energy flowing through the body is recycled on this earth. Cosmic energy continues to sustain your mind, soul and spirit in another dimension.

Right now, as you're reading, as you're holding this book, say-feel-know this book is a condensation of Divine Presence.

Now, look around the room, say-feel-know every thing in the room is a manifestation of cosmic energy. Move from object to object.

Whatever you can see, touch, taste, smell and hear is a variation of cosmic energy.

Look at the space of the room. It is filled with air, the life giving oxygen we breathe. You cannot see, smell, taste, touch or hear it, yet it is there.

You know it because you breathe it. It keeps you alive. Say-feel-know, it also is a frequency of cosmic energy.

Divine Presence is ubiquitous - omnipresent. Whether in the room you're in now or on the other side of the galaxy, the cosmic energy is present.

The light shines bright
Illumines cosmic night;
Rays of universal flame
Noetic consciousness its name.

Stars reach across space
Sparkle on your face,
Eyes on fire,
Christ frequencies inspire.

Sunshine bathes the sky
Getting an energy high,
Time is standing still
Through light's windowsill.

Light Wave 1

You Can Feel Divine Presence

Divine Presence is with you, in you and through you at all times. This is true whether you're conscious of it or not.

By learning to tune into Divine Presence, cosmic energy, you will feel its uplifting, calming, regenerative force.

Divine Presence is not exclusively the treasure of some future heaven. It is here now; and it is available to you. All you have to do is place your attention on it. At once it flows through mind, body and aura.

By placing your attention on Divine Presence, I do not mean thinking about it. I mean focusing steadily on cosmic energy. I mean being receptive to its flow, current, vibration and wavelength.

One way to tune Divine Presence in is to imagine yourself a radio. Your mind is dialing in the frequencies of divine energy, the music of the spheres. Your tuning, your focus must be precise. Let go of the static of extraneous thoughts.

Practice every day tuning into Divine Presence. At first, you may feel nothing. Still, you are tuning it in; you are just not conscious of it.

With persistent practice, you will sensitize your feelings to its continuous presence. In the beginning, the feelings will be vague. It will seem like you are feeling something, but you will not be sure what.

Gradually, the feeling of Divine Presence will be definite. You will feel a definite uplifting cosmic energy. You will feel renewed. Harmony, peace and love will fill your soul. Eventually, the mere thought of Divine Presence will be followed by coursing currents of divine energy. You will feel a deep reverence for everything and everyone. You will know and feel the Divine Presence permeating everything and everyone. You will desire to live in The Presence as much as you can.

Whenever problems and difficulties confront you, tune to the Divine Presence. In its peace you will know what to do. It is your true companion and guide.

Silent sounds echo through space,
Cosmic ripples and lace,
Intergalactic stellar weave
From second to second breath.

Void is fullness of presence,
God's eternal essence,
Formless time,
Cosmic mime.

Darkness, cradle of night
Expanded out of sight,
Yet ever within you
Continuously creating anew.

Light Wave 2

Separating From Divine Presence

Everything and everyone is intimately integrated and connected. This vast oneness is the Divine Presence.

Nothing and no one is separate from the oneness of Divine Presence. If anything or anyone were separate from Divine Presence, there would no longer be a oneness.

Contrary to truth, most men, women and children today think, feel, image and behave as if they are separate from Divine Presence.

Often, when using words in speech and thought, shortsighted intellectuals deny the existence of Divine Presence. Whether agnostics, atheists or unbelievers, verbal static prevents them from tuning into the source and sustenance. Nevertheless, The Presence is with them, despite their word juggling.

For varied reasons, many people feel alone, alienated - cut off from society, life and Divine Presence. This feeling is a lie, a deluded identification. In order to feel connected again, they must practice The Presence.

The imagery projected by television, film and magazines leads millions to imagine themselves separate personalities. The goal of these false godlings is to reach stardom in show business. The image of a self-separate personality leads to unbalance, unsane living.

The behavior of untold millions betrays their false belief -- I am separate from Divine Presence. Cheating, lying, stealing, violence and other anti-social behavior is the direct result of their false belief.

The suffering people endure in the attempt to "live" separately from Divine Presence is staggering. Yet, it serves a purpose: eventually, people return to a conscious connection with the limitless cosmic energy. The peace, harmony and beauty experienced as part of The Presence is true life.

Inner flame burning
Transmuting yearning;
Refined matter
Climbing the cosmic ladder.

Cool fire tuning,
Love force crooning,
Lifted to the heights
On galactic star kites.

Star blaze power
Transforms time's hour,
Matter-energy to light
Off on spirit's flight.

Light Wave 3

The Presence Will Relax You

You come home from work exhausted. You're edgy. You get annoyed easily. The pressures of the day were too much.

Instead of reaching for a drink or tranquilizer, tune to The Presence. It will relax you. It will rejuvenate you.

Here's how you go about it. Lie down. Breathe gently and slowly. Watch your breathing. Allow it to work naturally.

Next, place your attention on the Divine Presence. Feel a flow of cosmic energy through your mind and body.

Become aware of the fact that everything around you is Divine Presence. Know that the bed you lie on is a manifestation of Divine Presence. Know that the pillow your head is resting on is a configuration of Divine Presence.

Let go of extraneous, wandering thoughts. Reverently reach out to the infinite. Be receptive to the permeating vibrations of The Presence.

Feel it washing away all the pressures of the day. Feel the joyful relief when your cares and troubles evaporate from your mind.

Be eternally grateful for all the blessings The Source has bestowed upon you. Maintain your tuning. Commune happily with the Divine Presence.

After 20 or 30 minutes open your eyes. Get out of bed slowly. How do you feel?

Now for the rest of the evening you will feel more harmonious with those around you. They will feel a beautiful quality emanating from you. More love will circulate among family members.

Oftentimes, you will feel a glow in your face. You will smile inwardly. You will have a natural smile on your face. The Divine Presence has relaxed you.

Acknowledge The Presence

As you go about your daily duties, problems, frustrations and difficulties often arise. Naturally, it is important to know how to negotiate these sharp corners. Nevertheless, if you could acknowledge The Presence, even for a second, your problems will not seem as difficult.

You must realize for yourself that Divine Presence is not just a pretty word. Beautiful, religious sounding words are meaningless in and of themselves. True, they sometimes generate positive feelings, but they do not give you a direct experience.

Divine Presence can be experienced. Presence permeates your body and mind. In less than a second, you can focus your attention on it. And, eventually, in another second feel It's living energy.

It only takes a few seconds to acknowledge The Presence. Placing your attention on cosmic energy 10 times a day will take you less than a minute.

One minute during the work day to remember the source of life, breath and consciousness is certainly not too much to ask. The benefits will far outweigh the efforts.

By acknowledging The Source, The Source will acknowledge you. Every action has an opposite and equal reaction. When you become more conscious of The Presence, The Presence becomes more conscious of you. You will experience The Presence in mini-doses during your few seconds acknowledgement.

Gradually, you will sense: the Presence is always with you. Your problems will seem to solve themselves. Your difficulties will rarely be insurmountable. Answers and ideas will pop into your head.

Light consciousness seer
Transmutes dark fear,
Ever present rays
Sings Christ's praise.

Vibration of white,
Radiant colored light;
Energy fields vast,
Future, present, past.

Tune beyond word,
Sounds of light heard;
Touch-feel know
Noetic frequency flow.

Light Wave 4

Continuous Living In The Presence

Call Divine Presence what you will. The list of names is endless. Religions and philosophies abound with different names for what cannot be named.

It is nameless. The vibrational wavelengths, the frequencies of divine force, cosmic energy are non-verbal. Words are not the actual experience.

You must first experience the vibrations of Divine Presence before your words about It take on meaning. So stop verbalizing about It too much. Learn to experience by practicing some of the methods described in this chapter.

As you feel-know that The Presence is with you, you will desire to live continuously in Its frequencies. It will become your guide, source, center and sustenance.

It will replace all false gods, false authorities and false heroes. It will be your expert. It will direct you to the information needed.

When you become unbalanced, when you have lost your center and tuning, your consciousness will return to the spiritual source. Life will well up in you, an internal, eternal fountain of youth.

The feeling of slow, plodding clock time will disappear. Time will seem to flow more smoothly. In fact, time will seem to pass quickly.

Since your tuning is more on the eternal, time seems to zoom by. When you're identified with self-separateness, time plods along. Boredom then sets in. Boredom is a sure sign that a person has lost his center and source.

Live in The Presence continuously. You do not have to wait for special moments, times of the day or week. It is here, now. Simply put your attention on it.

Whatever you are doing at any given moment, remember The Presence. On the way to work, during work, after work, The Living Presence is with you. Even as you're doing the simplest tasks, you can tune to the Presence. In fact, it will improve the quality of your actions.

The joy, the peace, the stability experienced by living in The Presence is beyond words. Still, it is not beyond you to experience. A mere attentive focus of the mind in a receptive state and The Presence is an experience.

Star Stuff everywhere,
Vibrating here and there;
Intelligent light,
Visible and beyond sight.

Things are solid flame,
Energy without name;
Brilliant to mind's eye,
Time frame zipping by.

Matter is frozen fire
Not lifeless mire;
Ripples of radiant space,
Full of divine grace.

Light Wave 5

Summary

1. Divine Presence is Cosmic Energy.
2. Say-feel-know every thing is a manifestation of Cosmic Energy.
3. Divine Presence is here-now, and it is available to you.
4. Tune to Divine Presence by imagining yourself as a radio.
5. Eventually, the mere thought of Divine Presence will be followed by coursing currents of Cosmic Energy.
6. Whenever problems and difficulties arise, tune to the Divine Presence. It is your true companion and guide.
7. Nothing and no one is separate from the oneness of Divine Presence.
8. People suffer because they try to live separately from Divine Presence.
9. In order to relax tune to Divine Presence.
10. Acknowledge the Presence and your daily problems will not seem as difficult.
11. The Presence is always with you.
12. The frequencies of Cosmic Energy are non-verbal.
13. Experience the vibrations of Divine Presence then your words about it will take on meaning.
14. Tuning to The Presence will improve the quality of your actions.
15. The joy, the peace, the stability experienced by living in the Presence is beyond words; yet it is not beyond you to experience.

Chapter 2

Spiritual Science

What Is Spiritual Science?

Spiritual science is the study of vibrations, frequencies, energies, forces and fields, especially in relation with human growth. Spiritual science investigates these invisible influences so knowledge will be available to those who want to use it for spiritual growth.

Spiritual science is interested in developing methods, systems and exercises to assist others with balanced integration into the worlds around them. Of special interest in today's drastically shifting world is -- how to maintain a spiritual tuning in the midst of materialistic static.

Spiritual science differs from the traditional exact sciences such as physics, chemistry and biology. The exact sciences rely on precise observations and measurements. Rarely does it include the influence of the experimenter on the experiment.

In spiritual science, experiment and experimenter are inextricably bound together. There is a continuous interaction between the two. The frequency level of that interaction determines the level of the result.

For example, in spiritual science there is investigation and participation in the peaceful frequencies achieved in meditation, prayer and relaxation. There is a continuous interaction between the person meditating, praying or relaxing and the vibrational level a particular person is on at any given moment. Therefore, the results will always be more or less different within a certain range of similarities.

If a person has a well-trained skill in concentration and is familiar with the peaceful frequencies, the results will be on a quality level. On the other hand, if a person has difficulty concentrating, even for a few seconds, and they have not experienced the peaceful state, the results may not be on a quality level.

> *Flickers in space,*
> *Members of a light race;*
> *Conscious beings,*
> *Cosmic scenes.*
>
> *Intergalactic flames*
> *Without human names;*
> *Radiant conscious light,*
> *Iridescent white.*
>
> *Bright flashes flare,*
> *To eyes, unbearable glare;*
> *Bolt across cosmic night,*
> *Flexing star might.*
>
> *Light Wave 6*

Spiritual Science Is New Age Religion

There are cycles of time where certain points of view prevail. During the last 2,000 years, faith and belief have been the watchwords. Beginning now and continuing for approximately the next 2,000 years, knowledge and self-knowledge will be the emphasis.

Traditional religion's base their existence on the revelation of one man. His experience and message are taken by his followers as truth. By believing and having faith in that truth the follower could achieve some measure of salvation.

Despite religion's reign, science smoldered and flickered in the background. Now, as a New Age begins, it is wearing the crown, its fires are flaming.

Science seeks knowledge. It does not want belief; it insists on knowing. Because of this viewpoint, people do not want to believe in someone else's experience; they prefer to know about their own. The main emphasis of science so far has been observing and learning about matter, energy and things. Gradually, this scientific method will be used in observing and learning about oneself.

Self-knowledge is the first step in spiritual science. It is where science and religion meet. Out of self-knowledge a person not only learns about himself but learns about others.

As a person learns more about others his self-knowledge broadens and he begins to see where he saw nothing before. He begins to sense invisible energies of a higher order. Experiences of other dimensions open up to him.

At that point, for most people, guidance will be of great benefit. Someone who knows and practices spiritual science can help guide the budding knower.

Just as the exact sciences are based on certain natural laws, spiritual science or New Age religion is based on specific spiritual laws. The neophyte must learn and apply them before he can be called a spiritual scientist.

> *Light beam bright*
> *Blinds human sight;*
> *Opens godling eyes,*
> *Sees deluded lies.*
>
> *Illumines space-time,*
> *The light-man's climb;*
> *Weightless star-walk,*
> *Silent mind talk.*
>
> *Oscillating waves*
> *Through atomic caves;*
> *Alive with light,*
> *Super-radiant white.*
>
> *Light Wave 7*

Some Of The Laws Of Spiritual Sciences

Any science, on whatever level, must be based on laws. A law is an event or process that repeats with predictable regularity. For instance, if you throw a baseball you know without a doubt it will fall back to the ground. In physics this predictable result is called the law of gravity.

There are numerous laws in spiritual science. This comes as a surprise to many people. Most unjustly believe spirituality is indefinite, vague and borders on the mystical. In reality, it is based on laws as dependable as the law of gravity.

What follows is a brief outline of only four laws of spiritual science. There are many, many more. The four I have chosen can be verified by you through experience.

They are:
1. The Law of Rhythm
2. The Law of Gratitude
3. The Law of Love
4. The Law: Energy Follows Attention

The *Law of Rhythm* refers to the wave motion, up-down, in-out process of reality. Notice you cannot survive beyond a few minutes without breathing, a rhythmic activity.

Life from the stars to the atoms exists according to exact rhythmic patterns. You and I are integrated in the vast scheme of things, energies and consciousnesses. We too must live rhythmically, otherwise we lose our spiritual tuning.

More On Spiritual Laws

The *Law of Gratitude* can be defined as the thankful acknowledgement of infinite substance and intelligence.

Whenever something wonderful comes to you be grateful. Whenever life's necessities come to you be grateful. Practice gratitude every day.

When you become upset, disappointed or depressed turn your attention to thankfulness. If you persist your disappointment or depression will leave you. You will feel renewed, calm and at peace with the world.

If these claims seem ridiculous, amazing or unbelievable test them for yourself. For one week practice gratitude. At every opportunity be grateful, especially when you're disturbed about something.

The *Law of Love* is more popularly known as the golden rule, do unto others as you would have them do unto you.

When you treat others as you would like to be treated, love, respect and goodwill are generated. Wonderful, caring, loving things happen to you. You then pass those loving feelings on to others. You radiate love.

Put the Law of Love into practice. Treat others with respect and goodwill. Notice the flow of love, friendly words and respect which flows back to you.

Energy follows Attention is another spiritual law that can easily be tested by you. Choose an object. Place your attention on it. Your energy follows your attention.

Place your attention on eating. Do you notice your hunger? Do you want to get up and walk to the kitchen?

Now quickly place your attention on watching television. Hold it there. Notice how you begin to forget about being hungry. Your energy is following your attention.

By changing your focus you change the flow of your energies. If you are thinking negatively, you can stop simply by placing your attention on positive thoughts. It may take some practice to change from negative to positive quickly, but it can be done.

Galactic star-jewels,
Nuclear fire-pools;
Birth, life, death,
Cosmic rhythmic breath.

Light year arms,
Spiral charms;
Star-stuff rays
On cosmic sea bays.

Nuclear fusion,
Space-flame explosion;
Erupting gas,
Concentrated mass.

Light Wave 8

Becoming A Spiritual Scientist

First and foremost a spiritual scientist does not rely on the revelations of another. Instead, he or she investigates, experiments and tests. As a result, the spiritual scientist knows by experience. Belief in what someone says is not swallowed as truth.

Truth is relative depending on the perspective and perception of the observer or experimenter. Realizing and understanding this point, the spiritual scientist respects other views. When someone sees an event or process entirely different, the spiritual scientist avoids thinking and speaking along the frequencies of "wrong" versus "right".

A more thoughtful and considerate attitude is adopted: the other person has a right to their view. You respect it, but you do not believe or disbelieve. There is insufficient data. You will have to look further, gather more facts.

You cannot become a fully trained spiritual scientist overnight. Years of determined, rhythmic and steady development are required.

The body must be healthy and in repose. The emotional nature must be calmed, under control but not repressed: The mind must be cultivated, well-rounded and at peace. The connections to the spiritual frequencies must be established and steady.

The training is as difficult, if not more difficult, than needed to become a physicist, astronomer or chemist. The rewards are equal to, if not greater than, those experienced by the exact scientist.

This does not imply in any way that the spiritual scientist is superior or separate from the exact scientist. In fact, spiritual scientists include the exact sciences in their studies.

The measure of a spiritual scientist's growth is the degree of knowledge he has integrated into his daily life. Knowledge must be followed by conscious application. Gradually the application becomes part of the spiritual scientist's lifestyle.

> *Tune to conscious light,*
> *Removes the veil from sight;*
> *Spiritual uplifting,*
> *Energy shifting.*
>
> *Stop automatic thinking,*
> *Begins cosmic linking;*
> *Let go emotions drain,*
> *Quiet the reptile brain.*
>
> *Steady light reception,*
> *Transforms deception;*
> *Conscious spirit being,*
> *Star eyes seeing.*
>
> *Light Wave 9*

Branches Of The Tree Of Spiritual Science

Spiritual science is a limitless science. At present, there are numerous branches on the tree of spiritual science. Many of the branches have been named and investigated.

The following is a list of sciences within spiritual science. Each is a lifetime study/application, if not several lifetimes:

1. The Science of Consciousness
2. The Science of Wisdom
3. The Science of Light
4. The Science of Living
5. The Science of Mind
6. The Science of Health and Healing
7. The Science of Synthesis
8. The Science of Creativity
9. The Science of Cosmology
10. The Science of Semantics
11. The Science of Symbols
12. The Science of Transformation and Transmutation
13. The Science of Regeneration

Let's look briefly at the science of health and healing and the science of semantics.

Today holistic medicine has become popular. The holistic health movement takes into consideration the entire person -- spiritually, mentally, emotionally and physically.

Holistic health is the beginning of the science of health and healing. The other major tenets of this science are:

1. Negative thinking is the seed of dis-ease.
2. A depleted energy level is an invitation to dis-ease.

The science of semantics has had a resurgence during the twentieth century. Alfred Korzybski's *Science and Sanity* outlines many of the main points of this science.

Here are a few of those points:

1. The word is not the thing.
2. X_1 is not X_2 is not X_3 ...
3. Senses first, mind second.
4. Structure is the only content of knowledge.
5. The either/or two-valued orientation is replaced by the infinite valued orientation.

> *Light-thought-feel,*
> *Pain-sickness heal;*
> *Circulating health,*
> *Spiritual wealth.*
>
> *Calm storm emotion,*
> *Drink light's potion;*
> *Psychic turmoil cease,*
> *Radiate peace.*
>
> *Put out hot desire*
> *With light's cool fire;*
> *Awaken conscious will,*
> *Instinct's impulse still.*
>
> *Light Wave 10*

Summary

1. Spiritual Science is the study of vibrations, frequencies, energies, forces and fields, especially in relation to human growth.
2. In Spiritual Science experiment and experimenter are inextricably bound together.
3. Self-knowledge is the first step in Spiritual Science. It is where science and religion meet.
4. Just as the exact sciences are based on certain natural laws, Spiritual Science, New Age Religion, is based on specific spiritual laws.
5. A law is an event or process that repeats with predictable regularity.
6. The Law of Rhythm refers to the wave motion, up-down, in-out process of reality.

7. The Law of Gratitude can be defined as the thankful acknowledgement of infinite substance and intelligence.
8. The Law of Love is more popularly known as the golden rule, do unto others as you would have them do unto you.
9. Choose an object. Place your attention on it. Your Energy Follows Your Attention, another spiritual law.
10. A spiritual scientist does not rely on the revelations of another.
11. Truth is relative depending on the perspective and perception of the observer or experimenter.
12. The measure of a spiritual scientist's growth is the degree of knowledge he or she has integrated into daily life.
13. Spiritual Science is a limitless science.

Chapter 3

The Science of Consciousness

What Is Consciousness?

Consciousness is a state of acute awareness. It is not superficial everyday awareness, for example, when you see a wall, a tree, a car, etc.

When you are acutely aware, conscious, you see more deeply. You sense more than the thing; you sense-feel a quality, a vibration, an energy from whatever you're noticing.

Superficial awareness can be compared with two dimensions, length and width. Consciousness can be compared with three dimensions: height, width and length, and four dimensions: height, width, length and the force-field (energy-field).

The experience of being conscious goes beyond four dimensions. In fact, it continues awakening from one level to another as you unfold your being.

To be conscious implies an effort of will. We are not automatically conscious. There must be a steady, rhythmic, flexible effort. Notice, observe, be attentive.

Each day the effort must be renewed. Look, listen, smell, touch, feel. Sense without thinking.

Thinking is not being conscious. Becoming conscious that you are thinking and what you are thinking about can lead you to being conscious.

When you are conscious you will feel more alive, more energy. People and things seem more alive, or, in some cases, less alive.

Consciousness is cool, non-reactive, keen and attentive. Consciousness is aware of connections and relations. Consciousness searches out blind spots and shines a light.

Why Become More Conscious?

Becoming more conscious from day to day, from year to year is a natural process. To remain unconscious is to stagnate and die.

In order to grow, in order to be alive in the present, it is necessary to be conscious. You connect with the environment, you sense the world around you when being conscious.

Drifting aimlessly in a state of oblivious unconsciousness usually dooms a person to slavery. There can be no freedom for the unaware.

What is meant by freedom? Here it means the ability to choose a course of action, of thought, of desire and so forth. When a person is conscious he or she is liberated. The wider the consciousness the greater the liberation.

When you or I are unconscious in any area or situation, we have little or no freedom. We act, think, speak automatically, mechanically, impulsively. We do not choose to act in a certain way. The action drives us along unbeknown to us.

Becoming more conscious is worth the effort. New vistas open. Undreamed of opportunities come your way.

The more you become conscious the more living becomes a fullness of joy, happiness and keen interests. You will see yourself differently. You'll awaken to new ideas, places, worlds and energies.

Becoming more conscious means participating and cooperating with a process greater than yourself. It is the inherent thrust of life to seek wider horizons, new vistas and more abundant opportunity.

Tuning to the Spiritual Frequencies opens to you as you grow in consciousness.

> *Love-light vibration*
> *Heartfelt sensation;*
> *Nurturing life,*
> *Dissolving strife.*
>
> *Love-light energy wave*
> *Calms desire's crave;*
> *Star-love flow,*
> *Cosmic being glow.*
>
> *Love-light feeling*
> *Body, soul healing;*
> *Ever wanting to give*
> *Each day you live.*
>
> *Light Wave 11*

Sensing Without Association

Most of us do not use our five senses on a conscious level. Naturally, we hear, see, smell, taste and touch every day. The question is, though: what is the quality of your sensing?

Let's say you see a car pass by or hear a bird singing. If you're unconsciously sensing you will not notice the color, age, make or driver of the car. If you're unconsciously sensing you will not notice the pattern in the bird's song, the direction or the distance.

Practice using your senses more consciously. As you sense, do not think; do not associate ideas, memories and plans.

Notice how associations come into your mind after seeing, hearing, tasting, smelling and touching. Practice sensing in the present. Let go of memories.

Associations oftentimes block us from experiencing life consciously, fully. You see a car pass. You think: "I used to have a car almost like that one." By associating you have traveled, momentarily, back into the past.

The unconscious habit of associating when sensing cuts a person off from the present dynamic energy world. By daily conscious effort you can break the association habit.

Every morning consciously activate, use each sense. Notice size, shape, color, design. Listen to every little sound. Touch with sensitivity. Try to detect every smell around you. While eating, savor every flavor.

To consciously sense without associations demands steady daily effort. With one or two half-hearted curious tries, little will be accomplished. Work at it; experience the adventure of conscious sensing.

Spark of light glows,
The mind learns and knows;
Dark veils drop away,
Dawn of a new day.

Mind-fires are burning
Life lessons learning;
Electric mind thought,
Spiritual light sought.

Noetic mind light
Opens inner eyesight;
Blind night-hell gone,
Spiritual rays dawn.

Light Wave 12

Consciousness: Beyond Likes And Dislikes

Have you ever noticed how automatically you like and dislike? Unconscious likes and dislikes can inhibit and stunt your natural growth.

Have you ever had the experience of saying you do not like something and later end up liking it? Sometimes our likes and dislikes are not accurate. In other words, if we experienced something we say we like or dislike we may find out we do not like or dislike it at all.

Begin observing your likes and dislikes. When you automatically push something, someone, some feeling or idea away, especially when it's forceful, you are unconscious.

By observing your likes and dislikes, you will become conscious of many facets of your character which were hidden before. Next, you may break a particular like or dislike by consciously not experiencing it or consciously experiencing it.

For the sake of example, let's say you like cherry-vanilla ice cream so much you have gained 20 pounds. Consciously do not go with the urge-like next time. Now notice how powerful the urge is. It may seem irresistible. Remain conscious and it will pass.

Choose a powerful dislike, say, not liking to grocery shop. Consciously go to the grocery store and buy your food. Feel the dislike urge automatically push you away. Remain steadily conscious and it too will pass.

Light wave, rise-fall,
Rhythmic sounds call;
Inner currents swirl,
Spiral energy whirl.

Knowledge-Wisdom-Love
Descending from above;
Fills the auric-field,
Builds a spiritual shield.

Light wave music feel,
Psychic unbalance heal;
Melody of love plays
Songs of light's ways.

Light Wave 13

Bare Attention

Practicing bare attention will increase and broaden your consciousness. But before we find out how to practice bare attention, let's describe what is meant by the words "bare attention".

Bare attention refers to a particular state of awareness; no extraneous thoughts, images or words pass or fixate in the mental field. The awareness is focused on what is, what is happening in the present.

All judgments, opinions, views and values are laid aside. There is no right or wrong, good or bad. In this aware state, consciousness becomes keen and acute.

In bare attention you notice what is needed to be noticed. Nothing, that is necessary to see, escapes your awareness.

Bare attention is a sustained state of consciousness. It requires continuous attentive effort.

Bare attention is characterized by emotional calm. One registers impressions but does not react either too positively or too negatively.

In order to practice bare attention hold your attention in the mid-forehead area. Begin looking in a neutral observing condition. You are not looking for anything in particular; you are not avoiding anything in particular.

Practice bare attention as you go about your day. Try to go through the entire day while in a state of bare attention.

Listen in bare attention; walk in bare attention; work in bare attention; eat in bare attention and so on.

Much will come to consciousness when you practice bare attention that you were previously unconscious of. Actions you have repeated a thousand times will seem fresh and new. Faces will come alive with new detail. Nature will stun you with its beauty and vitality.

Practicing bare attention will improve your powers of concentration. Sustained concentration will assist you in every area of your life: home, work and play.

Intellectual thinking
In psychic mire sinking;
Word identification,
False deification.

Spiritual mind tune,
Noetic light boon;
Non-verbal peace,
God-energy release.

Brilliant thinkers hide
Behind word pride;
Light beings pray
Beyond word bray.

Light Wave 14

Perceptive Awareness

Perceptive awareness is unaccompanied by word or image. When in perceptive awareness you see without associating a word or memory.

For example, you see a dynamic energy field, a manifestation of cosmic energy, called a tree. However, when you see it, you do not immediately think the word tree.

Instead, you remain on the non-verbal energy world level. You see the tree in wordless awareness, in perceptive awareness.

It may take you some time to master perceptive awareness. In fact, after trying it out, you may think or feel it's impossible.

Let's approach it from another angle. Pretend you are a movie camera. Observe, watch, see as a neutral filming movie camera. Do it throughout the day. Perhaps you'll experience a degree of perceptive awareness.

Next, listen without forming an image or word of what you are listening to. Every sound is a universal vibration. Hear-feel-know the vibration. Try not to make associations about the source of the sound.

Now repeat for the remaining three senses, taste, touch and smell. Practice each in turn without automatic associations.

Take note of the feelings and energies when in perceptive awareness. Sense-feel-know the energy-vibration-frequency of whatever you are perceiving.

Repeated practice of perceptive awareness will broaden, deepen and enhance consciousness. As was said at the beginning of this chapter, consciousness is a state of acute awareness. To grow as an individual, the first step is to become more conscious.

Superconscious light wave
Transforms how you behave,
From ignorant fool
To gnostic being rule.

Noetic spark fanned
By an angelic hand;
Cosmic connection,
Aura protection.

Intelligent flame
Your birthright claim;
Feel-know the light-sound,
To the light world bound.

Light Wave 15

Summary

1. Consciousness is a state of acute awareness.
2. To be conscious implies an effort of will.
3. Consciousness is cool, non-reactive, keen and attentive. Consciousness is aware of connections and relations. Consciousness searches out blind spots and shines a light.
4. In order to grow, in order to be alive in the present, it is necessary to be conscious.
5. Becoming more conscious means participating and cooperating with a process greater than ourselves.
6. Practice using your senses more consciously. As you sense, do not think; do not associate ideas, memories and plans.
7. The unconscious habit of associating when sensing cuts a person off from the present dynamic energy world.
8. Unconscious likes and dislikes can inhibit and stunt your natural growth.
9. By observing your likes and dislikes you will become conscious of many facets of your character which were hidden before.
10. Bare attention refers to a particular state of awareness; no extraneous thoughts, images or words pass or fixate in the mental field.
11. In bare attention you notice what is needed to be noticed.
12. Practicing bare attention will improve your powers of concentration.
13. When in perceptive awareness you see without associating words and/or images.
14. Repeated practice of perceptive awareness will broaden, deepen and enhance consciousness.

Chapter 4

The Science of the Subconscious

What Is The Subconscious?

The subconscious level of the mind holds, retains and maintains that which is received from the conscious mind. Whatever is repeated long enough and often enough becomes part of its activity.

What is recorded in the subconscious mind does not have to be done consciously. Before a person becomes conscious most of what is recorded is done unconsciously.

By using the prefix "sub" it is not intended it should imply lower or primitive. Rather, it should imply "not immediately in consciousness".

The subconscious is in charge of the instinctive side of living. It sends the necessary messages to the conscious mind depending on the circumstance.

When the body needs more food for energy it sends a message of hunger. When the body is in danger it sends a message of fight or flight.

A difficult life problem is often surmounted by memories stored in the subconscious. For example, you're not sure how to settle a dispute or argument. Suddenly, you receive a hunch - compromise! You give in a little; they give in a little.

In the past you settled arguments successfully by compromising. The subconscious remembers those successes. It sends a message to the conscious mind letting it know it can be successful again. By understanding how your subconscious works and consciously cooperating with it, much can be accomplished.

Many do not acknowledge the subconscious level of mind. As a result, they tend to be in conflict with it. This can be disastrous since the subconscious does not differentiate good from bad, positive from negative. It will act on your negative thoughts just as quickly as on your positive thoughts.

The subconscious is like a mirror. An unclear image will be distorted in the subconscious. A clear image will be perfectly reflected.

Observe yourself, your moods, feelings, desires and thoughts. Do you find they are unorganized, confused and scattered? If so, know your subconscious mind is reflecting those distortions and reacting to them.

In order to Tune consistently to the Spiritual Frequencies the subconscious mind must be reflecting clear information. Otherwise too much static and confusion is disturbing the conscious mind's steady tuning.

The nature of the clear information is critical. The information must be natural order and accurate to the actual territory. In other words, facts, not fantasies, align the subconscious steadily to the conscious and superconscious levels.

The subconscious mind reacts automatically to whatever is reflected into it. A negative thought is reacted on by the subconscious and reinforced. The subconscious will recall memories substantiating the negative thought.

A positive thought is also reacted to. The subconscious will activate constructive associations. As a result, the positive reinforcement will attract the positive events more quickly and efficiently.

Whatever goes into your mind, your feelings, your emotions, your desires goes into your subconscious. Learn to surround yourself with healthy, balanced and constructive thoughts, feelings and desires.

Chaotic emotion
And confused notion,
Low frequency force
Pulls you off course.

Daily life pressures
Robs light's treasures,
Prevents sane living
And conscious giving.

Tune to the light-field
Dark veil unsealed;
Feel Christ force flow,
Makes your soul glow.

Light Wave 16

The Attracting-Repulsing Force Of The Subconscious

A woman I knew called a taxi in order to get home from work. She was always afraid she would get a terrible driver; most times she did.

After telling me her problem, I suggested she see the situation differently. "See and believe," I said, "that you will attract only excellent, well-mannered drivers."

Over a period of several weeks she experimented with my suggestion. She was amazed at the exactness. Nine out of ten times when she visualized and believed she would attract a good driver, she did.

The attracting and repulsing force of the subconscious is awesome. Yet, very few have any idea of its existence, much less how to control it.

If there are certain negative events repeating over and over again in your life, chances are you are attracting it by your unconscious thoughts, feelings and desires. Reverse the way you think and feel about that life situation. See if there is any change.

By unconsciously attracting habitual negative events you are repulsing positive events. The slower rate of negative vibrations blocks us from Tuning to the Spiritual Frequencies. So it is a must to learn how to control your subconscious forces of attraction and repulsion.

Much can be accomplished along these lines by observing your automatic likes and dislikes. What you like you tend to attract and what you dislike you tend to repulse.

Automatic likes and dislikes often blind us to the present situation. Try to be a bit less automatic. From time to time, attempt doing something you dislike. Observe what you go through inwardly.

As far as likes go, put off a particularly compulsive like until another day. Also, notice your internal reaction. Do what you like more consciously.

Ask yourself why you like it so much.

Ride the star streams,
Dimensions beyond dreams;
Currents of wisdom,
Crystal light kingdom.

Feel the crown of glory;
Tells the Gnostic story,
Transmutes illusion,
Spirit-mind fusion.

Spark divine thought,
Cosmic consciousness wrought;
Radiant silent light,
Show the blind, sight.

Light Wave 17

Becoming Conscious Of Subconscious Tendencies

Whatever you are unconscious of controls you. For the most part this statement is accurate. Check it out for yourself.

Have you ever been ripped-off or taken for a ride? Has anyone sold you a bill of goods? Most of us have.

At the time we were unconscious. We did not know what was going on. We were being controlled. We were unconscious of certain insidious subconscious tendencies.

In order to maintain a flexible spiritual tuning you must be conscious of subconscious tendencies. Be willing to see truthfully, honestly and openly any negative subconscious influences that you may have, no matter how seemingly insignificant.

There is no need to label the tendencies as "bad". You are not interested in the right or wrong of it. Rather, you are simply seeking self-knowledge as a means to inner growth.

When you are unconscious of a negative subconscious influence, you are controlled by it. A roadblock inhibits your further growth along specific lines.

Once you see and acknowledge certain tendencies you begin to let go of them. You do not identify as strongly, as automatically. The power of those influences begin to lessen.

Slowly, then more rapidly, with persistent effort, you consciously control your subconscious tendencies. At that point, unscrupulous characters will not be able to manipulate and control you. You will know what they are trying to do and you will not identify.

Inhuman vibrations,
Hot hell sensations;
Bathe in cool light
Heals inferno's bite.

Dark mind horror,
Astral body gore;
Still the psychic storms
With lighted thought forms.

Icy verbal lie
A million people die;
Light reveals the fact,
A billion souls can act.

Light Wave 18

Uprooting Subconscious Habit Patterns

Once you have discovered and acknowledged your subconscious reactions, attractions, repulsions and tendencies you are ready to uproot and eliminate pernicious habit patterns. (See Chapter 19: The Science of Regeneration).

You will realize that many rigid habits drain precious time and energy from what you sincerely want to achieve. In order to uproot and eliminate these habit patterns you must gradually stop the attention, the energy and repetition.

A habit can only survive if you give it attention, energy and repetition. What steps must you follow to halt these from going into maintaining a habit?

First, every time you catch your mind focusing, fantasizing or thinking about a habit, change the direction of your attention. This may take considerable practice. Do not be discouraged if you are not immediately successful.

Be persistent. As time goes on you will be able to change your attention with ease. Remember, the only defeat is not to get back up and try again.

A particularly vicious habit will not want to die. It will assert itself in any way it can in order to survive. When you are tired or upset or when no one is watching, it will seize your attention.

Remain steadfast. Ask sincerely for help. Let the automatic pulls pass. You are the boss.

As you command your attention the habits will lose energy. Without energy they begin to die. If you do not water your house plants or your garden flowers, they will wither and die.

As you command your attention and the habits lose energy the repetitions will be further and further apart. Without repeated actions the habits have no life. Eventually, they disappear. They are behind you, a memory of the past.

> *Unconscious hate and greed*
> *The mindless code and creed;*
> *Tune to divine presence,*
> *Taste energy essence.*
>
> *Seismic anger waves,*
> *Instant fissure graves;*
> *Quiet the mind quake,*
> *Conscious tuning awake.*
>
> *Volcanic inner mood,*
> *Depressed black brood;*
> *Christ consciousness dispells*
> *The chaos of man's hells.*
>
> *Light Wave 19*

A Subconscious Aid To Spiritual Tuning

By working consciously with the subconscious mind you can refine your Tuning to the Spiritual Frequencies.

An excellent aid to spiritual tuning is the affirmation. An affirmation is a written statement which is read aloud or silently in order to encourage a specific experience.

As an affirmation is repeated, the subconscious mind reflects it and begins a process of attracting the experience desired.

Let's say you would like spiritual guidance regarding a particular pressing problem. Write an affirmation sincerely requesting your need.

For example: With all my heart and with all my mind I request Divine Guidance and direction regarding my problem. I sincerely ask that I be receptive and attentive to an answer or answers which may be given in whatever way is most wise.

Perhaps before going to sleep you wish to feel a closeness to the Source of Life. The following affirmation may be of service.

> *Oh Cosmic Light, Radiant, Vibrant*
> *and Brilliant, regenerate, transform*
> *and transmute the base substance of*
> *sense, desire and emotion into the*
> *luminous wavelength of balanced*
> *Christ Light. May every cell bathe*
> *in Light, may every thought bathe in*
> *Light, may my consciousness bathe in*
> *Light.*

Here's another affirmation which may be used upon waking:

> *May the Divine Substance nourish me*
> *from day to day. May the Light of*
> *Wisdom shine in my heart. May the*
> *Joy and happiness of daily life be my sustenance.*

If possible, compose your own affirmations; they will have more meaning to you. The subconscious will assist you in your request, especially when repeated with open, genuine sincerity.

I do not want you to gullibly believe affirmations are effective. Choose an affirmation and test it continuously for one week. What do you notice? If you are not convinced of its usefulness, forget it for awhile. Then, at a later date, test it again.

Frequencies of light-sound
Everywhere abound;
Radiant chords,
Light being lords.

Rainbow music, listen
See the colors glisten;
Feel the audible stream,
Beyond worldly dream.

Melody of hue and shade
In God's consciousness played;
Each universe a note
By God's hand wrote.

Light Wave 20

Summary

1. The subconscious level of the mind holds, retains and maintains that which is received.
2. The subconscious is in charge of the instinctive side of living.
3. By understanding how your subconscious works and consciously cooperating with it much can be accomplished.
4. The subconscious will act on your negative thoughts just as quickly as on your positive thoughts.
5. In order to Tune consistently to the Spiritual Frequencies the subconscious mind must be reflecting clear information. Otherwise too much static and confusion is disturbing the conscious mind's steady tuning.
6. Whatever goes into your mind, your feelings, your emotions, your desires goes into your subconscious. Learn to surround yourself with healthy, balanced and constructive thoughts, feelings and desires.
7. If there are certain negative events repeating over and over again in your life, chances are you are attracting it by your unconscious thoughts, feelings and desires. Reverse the way you think and feel about that life situation. See if there is any change.
8. What you like you tend to attract and what you dislike you tend to repulse.

9. Whatever you are unconscious of controls you.
10. Be willing to see truthfully, honestly and openly any negative subconscious influence.
11. In order to uproot and eliminate habit patterns you must gradually stop giving them your attention-energy.
12. As you command your attention the habits will lose energy. Without energy they begin to die.
13. By working consciously with the subconscious mind you can refine your Tuning to the Spiritual Frequencies.
14. An excellent aid to spiritual tuning is the affirmation. An affirmation is a written statement which is read aloud or silently in order to encourage a specific experience.
15. Let's say you would like spiritual guidance regarding a pressing problem. Write an affirmation sincerely requesting your need.

Chapter 5

The Science of the Superconscious

What Is The Superconscious?

The superconscious is a frequency band of knowledge, wisdom and love which can be consciously contacted, felt and experienced.

Let's use an analogy, an AM-FM radio. The AM band of frequencies symbolizes everyday consciousness - awareness of hunger, of actions, of sensory experience, etc. The FM band of frequencies symbolizes psycho-spiritual consciousness - awareness of intuitions, of thoughts, of rapports, of inner contacts and connections, etc. The highest frequencies on the FM band can be compared to the superconscious.

You can experience the superconscious energies just as you can experience music received through a radio. You simply have to learn how to tune in.

The superconscious is the intelligence behind, within and throughout your everyday consciousness. The superconscious functions according to specific, definite laws - not moral or man-made laws but universal, cosmological laws. The superconscious can be experienced as an energy, a force, a field, a frequency.

The superconscious is not a metaphysical concept, a misty high order abstraction. The superconscious is not a mystical fantasy, a religious escape from worldly activity.

To be superconscious implies a purposeful direction of will in accord with a universal pattern. It is a cosmic law that energy follows attention. To apply this law to specific situations in order to improve, to grow, to consciously help, reflects a degree of superconscious action.

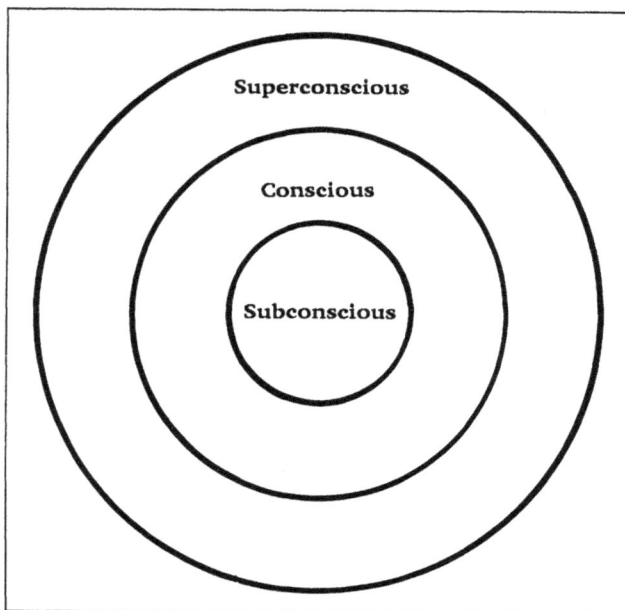

Figure 1: Concentric Circles of Consciousness

The superconscious, the conscious and the subconscious are related and interconnected as are concentric circles. The superconscious surrounds, encompasses both the conscious and subconscious.

The superconscious is experienced most directly through the conscious mind as long as there is not a lot of word-image static.
Unfortunately, today word-image static appears to be the norm so that we rarely experience the quiet repose conducive to superconscious experience.

In order to live a full, wholesome, well-rounded life you must incorporate, integrate superconscious experience. Although you are never really cut off from superconscious experience, your conscious mind censors those experiences, rejecting them altogether or neatly categorizing them as unreal, figments of your imagination.

Body pleasure and pain,
Mind pressure insane;
Chaotic force whirls,
Verbal noise quarrels.

Relax body stress,
Mental tension less;
Ordered energy wheels,
Non-verbal peace seals.

Think-feel-know the light,
Mind-body will not fight;
Force centers knowing,
Wordless sight growing.

Light Wave 21

Words Are Not Superconscious Experience

Many today mistake high sounding religious words said in a subservient tone, in a pseudo-devotional mood, for spiritual-superconscious experience. Mechanically spoken liturgy, intellectual para-psychological jargon and metaphysical epithets are mostly meaningless noise-words.

Let me tell you a true story. In the early 1970's I lived and studied in New York City. Each day I rode the subway to and from work. Often I used my subway time to apply-exercise my perceptive faculties.

One day there was a clergyman seated directly across from me clutching a black bible. He seemed to be in a state of intense inner talking. I realized he was praying to himself.

As I watched him, observed his psychological condition, I suddenly could psychically-telepathically hear him repeating the word-sound "God", "God" over and over again in his head.

Startled, I realized without a doubt he was not experiencing "God Energy" - cosmic energy - Divine Presence. His internal word repetitions of the verbal sound "God" acted as a kind of mental static which prevented him from feeling - experiencing Divine Presence.

True praying connects to the reality of superconscious frequencies of regenerate light. The clergyman was not truly praying. Instead, he was braying - making meaningless sounds disconnected from vital soul-vivifying experience.

The clergyman mistakenly identified the verbal sound "God" with actual experience. He falsely believed he was talking with God. In reality, he was manufacturing verbal noise sounds with fervent repetition.

Millions, hundreds of millions have fought and died, fought and died again, over these high sounding religious word-noises.

Words have their place. Words are symbols - road signs pointing the way if they are accurate road signs. You cannot experience a bend in the highway by seeing a sign which indicates a bend in the highway. (See Chapter 11: The Science of Semantics).

We must learn to experience the superconscious frequencies - Tune to the Spiritual Frequencies. It is a divine right that we feel these vibrations and eventually transfer identification to the superconscious band, force-field of dynamic reality.

There are specific, very definite ways and means of concentration and attention so that we gradually, step by step, transfer our center to the superconscious field of experience. The following sections will be road signs pointing the way. Knowing the way is not going the way. Practice, practice, practice - then you will have a conscious experience. Then you will desire more conscious experiences of the superconscious levels. Then the seed will have been planted.

God energy feeling,
Every second healing;
Let go egotism,
Self-separate schism.

Universal life force,
Omni-present source;
Everything you see,
Part of the cosmic tree.

Pleroma of light,
Diamond star bright;
Superconscious function,
Polarity's junction.

Light Wave 22

Meditation And The Superconscious

Meditation is one means whereby you can experience superconscious frequencies. There are literally hundreds of different ways of meditating. Although there are different methods, they all, if they are constructive, point toward a similar goal.

Let's go to the root of the word meditation: med, middle, medium. The goal of meditation is to tune to the middle - the center. When you are centered you feel a strengthening - an awareness of centered energy.

Have you ever felt an inward strength when doing something you deeply enjoyed or when in the quiet serenity of nature? That is the feeling when you are centered.

The goal of meditation is to consciously induce that feeling of being centered.

Once you are centered, currents of vital force streaming from the superconscious field fill your present awareness. The result: a keener, clearer perception, direct cognition, telepathic sensing, a conscious direction of energy, a desire to remain centered in the superconscious field, etc.

The following is only one form of meditation. It may be conducive to your natural ways. If not, there are numerous other methods you might want to look into.

Find a quiet spot, a place you can return to from day to day or when time permits. Perhaps it's a favorite chair or couch. Regardless, choose a spot that feels comfortable.

Sit up. Relax. (See Chapter 10: The Science of Relaxation) Concentrate. If your attention wanders or if you feel fidgety, return to a point of concentration. For some it may take awhile to achieve this stage of superconscious meditation.

Eventually, you will master one-pointed concentration. (See *Functional Mind Training* by Greg Nielsen). Now feel higher consciousness, force and energy. If thoughts inadvertently pop into your head (mental static) don't shoot them down or fight them, instead let them dissolve or evaporate. Give them no value.

Continually steady yourself. Remain in your center. New knowledge will become available to you. Love, Wisdom, Understanding, Will, Compassion and Faith take on new meaning. You begin to experience these traits as streams of force coursing through you, coming to the fore at the opportune - needed - moment.

Transmuted desire
In the cosmic fire;
Heated emotion
Cooled by conscious motion.

Feel universal ray
Transform night to day;
Natural order change
Increases conscious range.

Tune to Christ-light
At first blinds the sight;
Swirling, churning force,
Change, your only course.

Light Wave 23

Tuning To The Superconscious

As we go about our daily activities we are tuning in and tuning out. When working you must concentrate on specific tasks. As long as you are performing that task you are tuning into it. Other tasks, channels of activity are temporarily excluded.

After work you must tune in the activities of going home, of eating dinner, of relaxing, of going to sleep. Most of us go about daily activities unconsciously. Through force of habit we tune them in and out automatically.

When it comes to tuning into superconscious activities there must be a conscious effort of will. We must purposely direct our attention to an invisible frequency world. If we maintain our concentration, fix our tuning, then we will begin to feel currents of higher force. These feelings will be definite and very real.

In order to tune to the superconscious frequencies the channels of the senses, the thinking, the emotions and physical activities are tuned out. The more they are tuned out the more you can tune in the light force.

You will know when you have connected with superconscious light. Generally, you will feel more buoyant, centered, perceptive, directed, regenerated, peaceful and strong.

One of the keys to successful superconscious tuning is the steadiness of concentration. If you find your thoughts flitting like bumble bees from flower to flower, your mental body is out of control.

You are probably overly identified with words and images. Automatic words and images coupled with automatic emotions act as static on the superconscious channel.

To reduce the static, gradually stop identifying so intensely with words and images. Practice inwardly letting them go. Detach yourself from them. Observe them but do not give them value.

Realize that automatic identification with thoughts and pictures is a habit. A habit can be broken. It can be broken by having a strong desire to do so and detaching and redirecting your attention and,therefore, your energies.

Once you can consciously detach the flow of energy from mental static the superconscious channel opens. The superconscious transmissions which are continuously being emitted can then be consciously received, felt, experienced. Tuning to the superconscious is a skill that can be cultivated. Determined steady practice will open a whole new world of experience.

A special note: If you find strong skepticism and powerful doubt assert themselves while reading about these possibilities, try not believing or disbelieving. Assume a scientific stance. Experiment thoroughly with the techniques suggested. Reserve judgement. See what happens.

Automatic reactions,
Emotional fractions;
Pressure point pains,
Insanity gains.

Thought spin torture
Creates hell future;
False-image belief,
Realities reef.

Light circuit flow,
Cosmic contact glow;
Thought-emotion raised,
No longer crazed.

Light Wave 24

Time And The Superconscious

Once you learn to tune into the superconscious and feel-experience the high frequency energies, your time sense will change.

Clock time is an arbitrary system of measurement based on the rotation of the earth on its axis. When you're bored, depressed or impatient it seems like it takes forever for time to pass. On the other hand, when you're having a good time, happy and positive, time seems to go by quickly.

Besides clock time there is biological time and psychological time. Biological time has to do with the body's natural rhythms like breathing and digestion. Psychological time has to do with the psyche's rhythms like thinking, feeling, desiring and emoting.

Superconscious experience is characterized by a quality of timelessness, the absence of time. Just as it's difficult if not impossible to describe what sugar tastes like to someone who has never tried it, so too it is difficult to explain the timeless quality of superconscious experience.

Nevertheless, let's give it a go. As you register and feel higher currents of light, love and wisdom the mental faculty is still and the body is more relaxed. A kind of "psychological suspended animation" occurs. There is only the vast present.

The vast ever present now can be described as a pleroma of both potential and kinetic energy. All activity is universal motion. All potential activity is present in universal seed form, as archetypes.

Once you experience the timelessness of superconscious currents, clock, biological and psychological times seem less important. Still, you continue to live your daily life in accordance with these time frames. The difference is, though, you do not give them excessive value.

When light waves fade,
Dark waves braid;
Black chaos thought
With emotion wrought.

Web of daily rush,
Caught in the mind crush,
Then the spirit star
Flickers from afar.

Turn from dark to light,
Mind-tune, spirit might;
Flame fanned full,
Divine force-field pull.

Light Wave 25

Guidance From The Superconscious

At any of the world's busy international airports it is virtually impossible for a pilot to land without precise assistance from air traffic controllers. The pilot does not see from the wide perspective of those in the control tower.

The controllers, using radar and computers, keep track of distances and altitudes of all aircraft within the vicinity. The pilot, on a clear day, can keep tabs on only a few aircraft. During inclement weather or at night, a pilot is lost without assistance.

Guidance from the superconscious is similar to the guidance received from air traffic controllers. The superconscious has a wider view of your life situation than does the conscious mind. As a result, if you can contact and maintain communications with the superconscious you are likely to have less conflict, difficulty and suffering.

During a severe snow storm a pilot maintains communications with the control tower. If his radio were to fail, chances are he'd have to make an emergency landing. Suffering, destruction and lost lives could result.

Again, comparing your relationship with the superconscious, you particularly want to maintain communication with the superconscious during difficult life situations. Guidance in the form of intuitions, hunches, feelings, sudden insight, and knowings could provide the precise information needed to avoid unnecessary suffering.

Once the conscious mind works effectively with the superconscious mind, the impressions given the subconscious mind are accurate maps of reality. Accurate maps of reality, of energy-events, means you will be able to handle those events with greater ease.

The superconscious mind knows, understands and loves. It's not limited by rigid concepts, obsessive habits and emotional reactivity. It operates according to universal laws, not according to man-made laws. It is more interested in divine rights as opposed to human rights.

For example, it's a divine right to grow spiritually. The superconscious will always indicate how you can grow spiritually, even if it appears to be against what are defined as human rights. There are times when what's right for you appears wrong to most everyone else.

Cultivate your superconscious contacts and communications. Life will then unfold with the delicate ease of a flower.

> *Feel the mighty flow,*
> *Winds of spirit blow,*
> *Transforms apprehension,*
> *Glorious ascension.*
>
> *Feel the mighty light,*
> *Spirit's heavenly flight;*
> *Transmutation,*
> *Regeneration.*
>
> *Feel the mighty Christ-force*
> *Stream from the cosmic source;*
> *Brings light to black,*
> *Hope to lack.*
>
> *Light Wave 26*

Summary

1. The superconscious is a frequency band of knowledge, wisdom and love which can be consciously contacted, felt and experienced.
2. You can experience superconscious energies just as you can experience music received through a radio.
3. The superconscious functions according to specific, definite laws - not moral or man-made laws but universal, cosmological laws.
4. Many mistake high sounding religious words said in a subservient tone, in a pseudo-devotional mood, for spiritual - superconscious experience.
5. Meditation is one means whereby you can experience superconscious frequencies.
6. Once you are centered, currents of vital force streaming from the superconscious field fill your present awareness.

7. When it comes to tuning into superconscious activities there must be a conscious effort of will. We must purposely direct our attention to an invisible frequency world.
8. In order to tune to the superconscious frequencies the channels of the senses, the thinking, the emotions and physical activities must be tuned out.
9. Superconscious experience is characterized by a quality of timelessness, the absence of time.
10. The superconscious has a wider view of your life situation than does the conscious mind. As a result, if you can contact and maintain communications with the superconscious you are likely to have less conflict, difficulty and suffering.
11. Once the conscious mind works effectively with the superconscious mind the impressions given the subconscious mind are accurate maps of reality.
12. The superconscious mind knows, understands and loves. It's not limited by rigid concepts, obsessive habits and emotional reactivity.
13. The superconscious will always indicate how you can grow spiritually, even if it appears to be against what are defined as human rights.

Chapter 6

Mind: The Tuner

What Is The Mind?

Here we are going to use the word mind as it refers to the mental-reasoning faculty. The mind function is thinking. But what do we mean by thinking?

Thinking involves many functions and levels. Here are a few:

Functions

- Analysis
- Synthesis
- Comparing
- Contrasting
- Deductive Reasoning
- Inductive Reasoning
- Ordering
- Etc.

Levels

- Negative Thinking
- Emotional Thinking
- Automatic Thinking
- Scientific Thinking
- Spiritual Thinking
- Etc.

The mental energies can be applied constructively or destructively depending on your motive and attention. Selfish, egocentric, competitive desires generate destructive thinking. Thoughtful, understanding, wise motives generate constructive thinking.

Using your awareness, the conscious function of the mind, you must take note of your intentions. If you discover, uncover selfish motives, then you must take steps to change your focus of attention away from the negative intention. You must next take care not to allow your mind to begin a process of selfish thinking. Nip it in the bud. Halt the flow of life energy along those lines.

By gradually becoming more and more conscious of mental activities the ability to keep it under control increases. For example, you will notice the stream of words and images moving through the mental field. Ask yourself, what do they mean? Why are they there? Where are they coming from?

You will begin to discover that some words and images are meaningless mental static; a waste of time and energy. Gradually, you will desire and learn how to turn mental activity on and off at will. Also, you will desire to base most all of your thinking on the facts, the actual energy conditions of a particular event.

Then, knowing that energy is dynamic and ever changing, you will not fix the facts forever. You will learn flexibility of mind. You will be willing to look and see anew. You will be willing to think and see anew. You will be willing to think differently based on a new set of facts - energy circumstances.

Gradually, as you harness the functions of the mind you will desire to use its functions in service of the higher. Mind will become the tuner and conscious channeler of higher energies.

Inner conflict rages,
Parts of us in cages;
Mind-thought tune,
Light behind the moon.

Past life pattern,
The strong hand of saturn;
Light dispells the dark
Leaving shadows' mark.

Letting go of old ways,
Letting in light rays;
The fight within each soul,
Not over till it's whole.

Light Wave 27

The Servant Of The Higher

Relative to the instincts, appetites and impulses the development of the intellectual faculty is most certainly a worthy achievement. Still, intellectual acumen is not the peak of human achievement. The true role of the mind is as the servant of the higher.

Unfortunately, the intellect's importance has been over-valued in the world today. It's balanced training is a must in our society. But to place such a great value on it to the exclusion of spiritual-intuitive growth means misuse of the intellect.

For the most part the scientific intellectual mind has served the materialistic pleasure-profit motive. The military-industrial complex: the chemical industry, the oil industry, the automobile industry, the computer industry - the list goes on and on - strives almost exclusively for more profit in the competitive marketplace.

The intellect has in many instances become so over-developed that some try to reason away spiritual realities, energies, frequencies and laws. This kind of false pride has bred a monstrous egotism with socially accepted selfish motives. Egotism is justified as being "perfectly normal".

Gradually, you must reorient your intellectual achievement realizing its rightful place is as a servant of the higher. Using the intellectual faculties to help bring about the channeling of spiritual energies is a goal you must strive for. The realization must come to each in his or her own time that: the mental energy is a condensation of spiritual energies functioning on the mental level.

Take care not to misunderstand what I've said. I do not mean you should use the mind for vague mystical pursuits or metaphysical verbal juggling. Train your intellect. Make your mind sharp.

What I am saying is: apply your intellectual skills to spiritual matters. Meditation, higher tuning, invocations, studying cosmic laws, writing and speaking of the spiritual frequencies are just a few of the ways mental and spiritual energies can be integrated.

Mental discrimination is invaluable when pursuing spiritual goals, when Tuning to the Spiritual Frequencies. You will not confuse one level of reality with another. You will not mistake psychic phantasmagoria with cosmological realities. Your mind will become a stabilizing influence each step along the spiritual path.

Limitless expanse,
A cosmic dance;
Nuclear fires,
Planetary pyres.

Feel divine connection,
Light is your protection;
Whistle a heavenly song,
It will make you strong.

The light is in your cells,
Listen to what it tells;
Fan it with your mind,
Light waves will unwind.

Light Wave 28

How To Let Go Of Inner Talking

Are you aware of inner talking? Did you know there is a steady stream of words and phrases moving through your mental center?

Stop reading for a moment. Look around your immediate environment. See without thinking. Avoid identifying with words or phrases entering the mental field. Are you able to sustain concentration in observation without inner talking? Most of us can not halt inner talking without considerable effort and practice.

Why slow down and be able to turn off inner talking? First off, mental word streams burn-waste enormous amounts of life energy. Secondly, if we are ever going to Tune to the Spiritual Frequencies consistently, we must eliminate the static of inner talking when necessary.

Now, how to turn off inner talking? First and foremost you must become keenly, acutely aware of your inner talking. To achieve this first step you must practice self-observation.

Begin by sitting quietly and trying to catch yourself word-image thinking. Try to observe the precise moment when your mental attention is captured by automatic inner thinking. Practice this exercise regularly until you can, at will, notice the words-images mechanically entering your mental field.

Next, you must practice not identifying with the word-image stream. Stand in neutral. The words and images are not you. You do not have to identify or believe the inner talking. Insist on not automatically identifying with words and images. Realize it's often a waste of precious life energy.

Gradually, you may discover how meaningless the inner talking is in most cases. It will begin to look and sound absurd and ridiculous to you. You'll probably begin to wonder why the word stream even happens and where it comes from.

Once you've learned to cut down on automatic identification with inner talking, practice turning your attention away from the mental field. Direct your attention to observation of what's happening around you, to the energy-things around you, to the people around you without associating. Automatic associations trigger inner talking.

Then practice directing your attention to the spiritual frequencies, to the supersubtle frequencies of consciousness. Feel those vibrations and forces.

If you have great difficulty letting go of inner talking hold your attention steady at a point between the eyebrows and take slow rhythmic breaths. This exercise will also re-direct your attention and also strengthen your will and concentration.

Worry, doubt and fear
Enemies of the seer;
Wisdom, love, light
Friends of inner sight.

A negative thought,
A black mood wrought;
Try rhythmic breath,
Emotions death.

Gripped by fright,
The body uptight;
Relax the tension,
Let go apprehension

Light Wave 29

How To Be Receptive

In order to use the mind to Tune effectively to the Spiritual Frequencies you must learn to be receptive. To achieve a receptive state three conditions are required:
1. Physical Repose
2. Emotional Calm
3. Peace of Mind

Physical repose means relaxation. Notice the tensions building up in your body especially in stressful situations. In particular, try to feel tensions behind the neck, the back, the jaw and in the legs. You must first become conscious of excess tension before you can let it go.

Once you know when and where you become tense you must practice relaxing. There are two forms of relaxation:

1. Passive Relaxation
2. Active Relaxation

You must master both in order to achieve physical repose at will. (See Chapter 10: The Science of Relaxation).

Passive relaxation refers to quiet inactivity while lying down or sitting. It's conscious rest and repose, especially when alone. For example, to relax the neck muscles rotate your head slowly first clockwise then counter-clockwise. Feel the tensions release. If you discover tensions in the face and jaw muscles massage gently with the fingers.

Active relaxation is not recognized as much as passive relaxation. Active relaxation means doing whatever you're doing with the minimum amount of effort. For instance, take any activity X, let's say washing the dishes; do it slowly, consciously and with no excess muscle tension.

True receptivity can not be achieved without practicing emotional calm. Tuning to the Spiritual Frequencies is virtually impossible as long as emotional conflicts and turbulence imprison our attention.

Emotional calm is a psychological state where automatic reactivity is reduced and eliminated. You rise above the emotional frequencies by not giving your hyper-reaction value. The less value you give emotional identifications, despite strong intellectual justifications, the less power they have over you.

Peace of mind is a state of wordless awareness. By stopping inner talking you can go a long way toward achieving peace of mind. Once the restless, relentless uncontrolled activity of the mind is stopped then the higher frequencies can be experienced.

When you simultaneously combine all three: physical repose, emotional calm and peace of mind, you are in a powerful state of receptivity. To the degree that you can hold the receptive condition is the degree to which you can sustain spiritual tuning.

When you're bone tired
And your mind is mired,
Tune gently to the light,
Feel quiet star might.

When you're down and out
You wanna burst and shout;
Breathe in peace,
Disappointment release.

When you're angry hot
And things are not;
Cool hell bent speech,
Listen to light waves teach.

Light Wave 30

Use The Mind For Tuning In

Once you've learned to steady the mental energies a new world opens to you. You can now experience the frequency-energy universe consciously and directly.

With your one-pointed sustained attention you can tune to any person, place, thing, event or process. By consciously tuning to a friend or loved one you will register-feel the quality of their psychological state. Or, if you prefer Tuning to the Spiritual Frequencies of your master-self, that possibility is available to you.

This dramatic change can be compared to a blind man living in a cave totally identified with his sensations of touch, smell, taste and hearing. He is unaware of the sense of sight or of a world outside the cave. Then one day he stumbles on the opening of the cave. He longs to explore the world outside the cave but knows he doesn't have the faculty necessary to survive. But as a result of his intense longing and desire he awakens the latent sense of sight and a new universe opens to him.

New opportunities come to one who learns to consciously tune in. By sensing where others are at, you will adapt what you say and do to maintain a harmonious flow with others. If you desire to go to a certain place at a certain time you will be able to tune into the energy quality of that place at that time. Now, if the energies are harmonious you go; if inharmonious you can decide not to go, thus avoiding a draining experience.

You bring your tuning skill into every area of your life. Here's a partial list:

1. Food
2. Shopping
3. Choosing a doctor, dentist, mechanic, etc.
4. Entertainment
5. Friends/Family
6. Job
7. Travel
8. Reading Material
9. Music
10. Etc.

Practice using your tuning in skills to improve the quality of these life areas. Self-knowledge grows by leaps and bounds by applying your tuning in capability on yourself. Tune into your:

1. Physical Health
2. Emotional State
3. Feeling Tone
4. Mental Field

5. Subconscious Blockages
6. Pressure Points of the Past
7. Spiritual Self
8. Etc.

As your tuning capacity grows, universal vistas open, time barriers fall away and unimaginable experiences become possible.

Measuring Length And Strength Of Tuning

Jim and Sal were partners in business. Sal had just been recently married and was on his honeymoon.

Jim ran things smoothly until one day he could not locate an important tax record file. The IRS needed the records immediately. Jim and the staff searched high and low for the file but could not find it.

It was absolutely imperative that he locate the file. Jim had to contact Sal somehow. He had no number or address by which he could contact him.

Jim heard about the possibility of telepathy by tuning into someone. In desperation he gave it a try.

Sitting at Sal's desk he began to concentrate on Sal - tune into him. He sent him the message to call immediately.

Jim tuned in, concentrating almost too much. After a couple of minutes he stopped sending Sal the message. He sat back in Sal's chair waiting to see what would happen.

Within 15 minutes the phone rang. Lo and behold, it was Sal.

Sal told Jim that while driving on the Interstate he felt a sudden pressure on his head and an irresistible urge to call the office. He said the force of the message was overpowering.

Sal told Jim where the file was. Consequently, the IRS received the information needed.

Two important points should be noted from this true story:
1. The Length of Tuning
2. The Strength of Tuning

These points are especially critical when tuning into others.

First, length. Learn to tune in for as long as necessary, no longer. Effective, efficient tuning is the key. If longer than necessary you waste precious time and energy.

In order to judge-measure length accurately you must become sensitive to the effects you're tuning has on both yourself and who you're tuning into.

Just as you know the difference between looking at someone and staring, you learn to differentiate precise tuning from too short or too long tuning in.

Secondly, strength. Measure the force and strength of your tuning. Jim underestimated the power of his concentration. He was too forceful in his telepathic tuning.

Sal could have been distracted from driving and gotten into an accident. Fortunately, no one was around since he was on the open highway.

Again, you must become sensitive to the force of your tuning. The mind knows no distance. Tuning is relatively instantaneous. Once your message is received, stop. There's no need to keep calling the person once they have answered.

Intelligent light,
Structured bright;
Evolved light being,
Cosmic queen.

Consciousness king,
Diamonds sing;
Guide the light
Through earth-bound night.

Prince of time,
Universal rhyme;
Cosmic clocks run
The galactic sun.

Light Wave 31

Summary

1. The mental energies can be applied constructively or destructively depending on your motive and attention.
2. By gradually becoming more and more conscious of mental activities, the ability to keep it under control increases.
3. As you harness the functions of the mind, you will desire to use it in service to the higher.
4. The intellect has, in many instances, become so over developed that some try to reason away spiritual realities, energies, frequencies and functions.
5. Most of us cannot halt inner talking without considerable effort and practice.
6. If we are ever going to Tune to the Spiritual Frequencies consistently, we must eliminate the static of inner talking when necessary.

7. In order to use the mind to Tune effectively to the Spiritual Frequencies you must learn to be receptive.
8. To achieve a receptive state three conditions are required: 1) Physical Repose, 2) Emotions Calm, and 3) Peace of Mind.
9. To the degree that you can hold the receptive condition is the degree to which you can sustain spiritual tuning.
10. With one-pointed sustained attention you can tune to any person, place, thing, event or process.
11. As your tuning capacity grows, universal vistas open, time barriers fall away and unimaginable experiences become possible.
12. Learn to tune in for as long as necessary, no longer.
13. Measure the force and strength of your tuning.
14. The mind knows no distance. Tuning is relatively instantaneous.

Chapter 7

Becoming an Energy Being

What Is Energy?

We live in an energy universe. Energy is vibration. Every thing, person and event in the universe has a rate of vibration.

So called "physical" things are energy, each with its particular frequency vibration. Scientists have broken down matter into its constituent atomic structures. Things are made up of atoms which are in turn made up of protons, neutrons and electrons, etc. Things are energy structures.

A person has a rate of vibration. Have you ever felt really positive or negative vibes from someone? At that moment you are consciously experiencing their energy level.

Thoughts, feelings, moods, attitudes, desires and emotions are frequencies of energy. Practitioners of biofeedback record the energy vibrations of thought, feeling and attitude on sophisticated electronic equipment. They are able to teach others to be aware of their energies and to control their direction.

Spiritual aspects of life have a rate of vibration, high frequency energy relative to most of us. Love, understanding, wisdom, patience, etc. are energies which can be consciously contacted, experienced and cultivated.

Daily events are the coming together of a multitude of energy currents. When the energies blend and mesh a constructive event occurs, (relative to the human sphere). On the other hand, when the energies conflict and clash destructive events occur.

To truly know what energy is we must avoid trying to give an ultimate definition. The effort will prove futile. Words, no matter how exact the scientific observations, are not energy.

To know what energy is it must be experienced consciously. As each of us grows psychologically and spiritually we experience energies which are new to us. As the realm of our experience widens so does the range of energies available to us.

Gradually, each will learn to raise, lower or hold steady his or her energy level. Raising your vibration, you avoid getting into sympathetic vibration with negative (relative to you) things, persons and events.

Naturally, we must learn to maintain a rate of vibration. Holding steady to an energy level instead of unconsciously flitting will give direction and stability to your life.

> *From the stress and strain,*
> *From the endless pain*
> *Emerges a light being*
> *On the cosmic scene.*
>
> *From the work and toil,*
> *From emotions boil*
> *Evolves a soul*
> *That's cosmically whole.*
>
> *From life and death,*
> *From the gasp for breath*
> *Comes the diamond light*
> *Through cosmic night.*
>
> *Light Wave 32*

We Are Not Just Physical Bodies

Most of us make a lot of unconscious assumptions about who and what we are. One of these is the false belief that we are our bodies. This has resulted in devastating consequences to each of us and to the world we live in.

The body is not a thing. The body is not a lump of hard matter. The body is a dynamic master system of inter-related systems. The body is a dynamic configuration of energy units.

Now, when we believe the body is matter there's the unconscious assumption that it is not vital and alive. After all, things are not conscious; they're just lumps of matter.

In reality, the body is teeming with vitality. It's various functions are amazing to behold.

The body is a dynamic energy system. But, still we are not our bodies. We are much more. We also experience thoughts, feelings and spiritual aspirations.

When we over identify with the body, thoughts, feelings and spiritual aspirations are given little attention. As a result, our interests revolve around physical needs alone: food, shelter, clothing, exercise, cosmetics, sex, etc.

Growing older, the body ages. For those overly identified with the body, aging can have a traumatic effect. Their whole image of themselves is wrapped up in their physical appearance. Each wrinkle is a new horror.

What can we do to offset our automatic identification with the body? Begin seeing-knowing that we are energy beings. We are dynamic energy beings in a dynamic energy world.

In fact, practice saying to yourself, "I am a dynamic energy being in a dynamic energy world." As you go through the day, repeat it often. Recondition yourself to the life-fact -- we live in an energy universe.

When you touch something say, "this is a configuration of energy units." When you touch your body or someone else's say, "this is a configuration of energy units."

Next time you observe yourself thinking and feeling, know that you are registering a frequency of energy. Know that in prayer or meditation, when you feel the peace from above, you are tuning to a spiritual energy.

Practice becoming an energy being until it is the only way you act, think, feel and speak.

The psychics tire,
Their egos mire;
The noetics grow,
They infinitely know.

The metaphysicians bray
With words they play;
When the noetic speaks
The student seeks.

The mystic drifts,
Offering phantom gifts;
The noetic ever gives
The steady way he lives.

Light Wave 33

Right Use of Energy: Two Axioms

Here are two axioms which if meditated on, memorized and applied to life situations will go far in helping you become an energy being.

AXIOM I: Whatever it is you are going to do, there is just so much energy available for a specific amount of time to fulfill (complete) that action (task) or complete a certain percentage of it.

AXIOM II: If you go beyond that certain amount of energy for a specific length of time, the activity inverts and a destructive use of energy results.

These axioms can be applied to any activity X. Let's fill in the X with an example.

You are starving. You must eat. You decide to go to a buffet where you can eat all you want.

Upon arriving, you go directly to the food line and fill your plate with gourmet delights. Starved as you are, you gobble the tasty treats in a couple of minutes.

You want more; it's so good. Back to the line. Fill it up. Back to the table. Gobble it down.

Now you are feeling full. A certain amount of time has passed and a certain amount of energy has been used.

Still, you want more. This time it's direct to the dessert line. A piece of pie, cake, ice cream, pastries; it all looks so good.

You are eating a little slower now. Even though you are stuffed, somehow you are going to force it down. There must be room for more good food.

Now you have gone beyond a certain amount of energy for a specific length of time. The activity has inverted. A destructive use of energy results.

You are so miserable after finishing what started to be a delightful gourmet treat that you feel sick. You cannot wait to get home and crawl into bed.

A positive experience has inverted into a negative experience by misusing energy and time. (The blend of the two may be labeled timergy).

Test the two axioms for yourself. With application you will gradually become sensitive to the precise amount of time-energy (timergy) to complete an action or a percentage of it.

Here is a list of suggested activities:
1. Physical
2. Emotional
3. Mental
4. Creative
5. Social
6. Financial
7. Spiritual

What happens to you when the timergy of these activities is just right? When the timergy is excessive?

Tune to inner light,
Makes thought bright,
Creative spark,
An eternal mark.

Tune to inner light
Let go feelings uptight;
Radiate peace,
Frustration release.

Tune to inner light,
Makes actions right;
A kind deed,
The spirit freed.

Light Wave 34

How To Channel Your Energy

Try this experiment. Focus your attention on your thumb. Hold it there. If your mind wanders, bring it back.

If you are able to sustain attention, what do you notice? What do you feel?

Those of you who tried this small experiment now have an experience in consciously channeling your energy. You have learned something about the first Law of Life Energy: *ENERGY FOLLOWS ATTENTION.*

Every function whether it's painting, thinking, meditating, etc. requires: 1. *Attention,* and 2. *Energy.* Whatever you accomplish in this life it will demand your attention and energy.

Now ask yourself where do you place your attention each day? Wherever you place your attention that's where your energy goes from day to day.

Use the *Eight-Spoked Wheel of Whole Living* as a guide to finding out where your attention-energy is focused (figure 2 on page 56).

1. Physical - Bodily action, sports, exercise, blue-collar work, etc.
2. Mental - Read, study, think, etc.
3. Emotional - Ups and downs, moods, etc.
4. Creative - The arts, etc.
5. Social - Relationships, gatherings, leisure activities, etc.
6. Financial - Making money, etc.
7. Regeneration - Self-improvement, change, etc.
8. Spiritual - Prayer, meditation, higher tuning, etc.

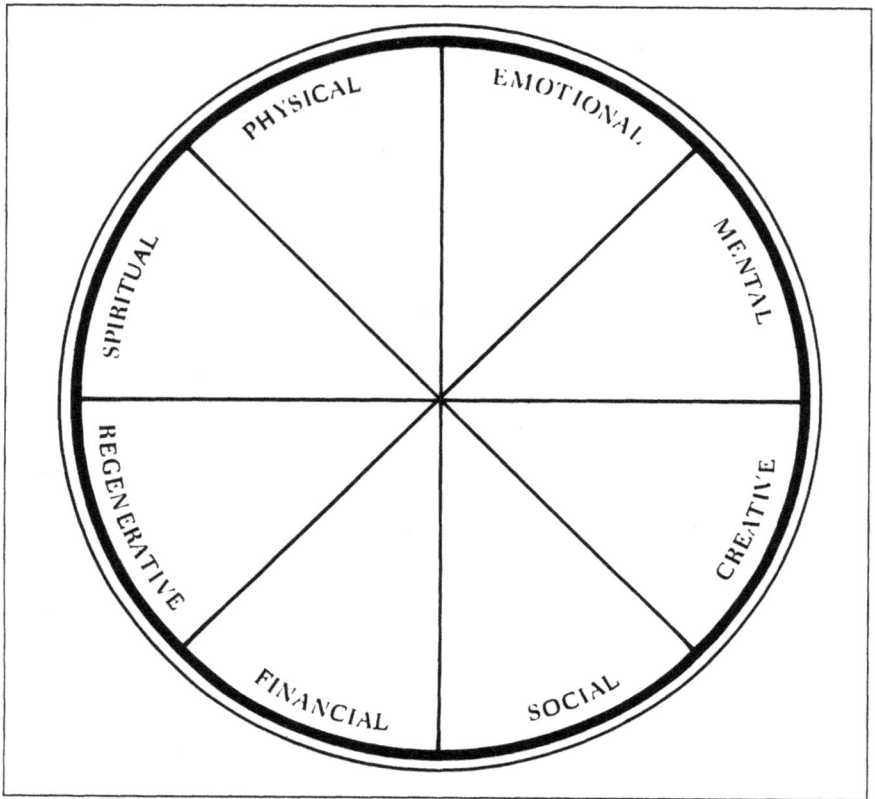

Figure 2: Wheel of Whole Living

Obviously these 8-life areas are interrelated indicated by the wheel. The purpose here for artificially dividing them is to help you become conscious. By becoming conscious of where you focus your attention and thus expend your energy, you take the first step toward purposefully directing your energy and, therefore, your life.

As you look at The Wheel of Whole Living think of:
1. Yesterday
2. Last Week
3. Last Month
4. Last Year.

Estimate as truthfully as you can how much of your life energy (in percentages) has gone into each of the eight areas yesterday, last week, last month and last year.

How To Experience Energy Vibrations

In order to consciously register and experience energy vibrations you must develop sensitivity. There are basically two kinds of sensitivity:

1. Automatic.
2. Conscious.

Automatic sensitivity is mechanical instinctive reactions to pleasure and pain. Conscious sensitivity is under your control. You choose to be sensitive. You turn it on and off.

When I say develop sensitivity, I'm saying develop conscious sensitivity.

Try this experiment. Go to your refrigerator and cupboards and take out various foods and condiments. Place a half dozen to a dozen items in front of you and sit down. Whatever is closed or shut, open.

Now take the first item. Let's say it's salt in a salt shaker. Remove the top. If you are right-handed cup your right hand slightly and bring all fingers into contact. The idea is to point the tips of your fingers and thumb directly over the salt.

Remember, everything is a configuration of energy units - the salt, the shaker, your fingers, etc.

Now, consciously sensitize the tips of your fingers so they are receptive to the energy emitted from the salt. Be sure to hold your hand close enough, within two inches.

Do you feel anything? What kind of sensation-energy are you picking up?

Repeat the "vibing" of all the other substances. Are you able to register the vibrations of some things more definitely than others? Do some seem to have a soothing vibration and others an irritating vibration?

When the experiment is over, be sure to consciously turn off the sensitivity in the fingertips.

Once you develop your "vibing" skill to a proficient level, practice vibing people. Naturally, you don't stick your hand into their face. Instead, you may lightly, not too intensely, sensitize your whole body. Consciously register an energy and quickly desensitize.

Once you have the sensitizing process thoroughly under your control you can remain sensitive to other energies as long as necessary, keeping in mind the two axioms of human energy.

Note the positive and negative energies you register from others. Where do you feel it? Do you feel a warmness in the heart? A slight stab in the stomach? Energized or drained?

When the body's strain
Numbs the brain
And dark moods hold
Freezes the fire cold;

When disappointment reigns,
A tyrant insane,
And negative thought flood
Destroys the blood;

Then with herculean will
Make thought-emotion still,
Grasp the diamond light
Til every cell has star might.

Light Wave 35

The Human Energy Meter

Balanced and measured use of energy results in a healthy, vital and wholesome life. Using the Human Energy Meter (figure #3, page 59) as a mind-tool you can discover where you misuse energies and improve your energy use.

Let's practice using the Human Energy Meter. Choose any activity: physical, emotional, mental, creative, social, financial, spiritual, etc. To illustrate, let's choose driving a car.

As you're driving, quickly visualize turning the Human Energy Meter on by pushing the right-hand button. Ask yourself how much energy on a scale of 0-10 you are using as you drive. See the arrow move up the scale to the appropriate number.

Remember to maintain acute attention to whatever you're doing while doing this exercise.

Now, if you're racing, mentally-emotionally reflected in a driving habit of zipping in and out of traffic while speeding, the meter will read 9 or 10.

If you're tired from a hard day's work and not paying strict attention to the road and other drivers the meter will read 1 or 2.

When expending too much energy, turn the reading dial down. Calm down, relax, become less intense.

When expending too little energy turn up the reading dial. Come to attention, get into the natural flow.

Sometimes you may have to turn the reading dial all the way down to zero, meaning: stop whatever you are doing and rest.

After using the Energy Meter for a few days you may discover that most of the time you register 8-9-10, tone yourself down. Habitually using too much energy is like killing a fly with a cannon. Turn your energy intensity down to precisely meet the needs of the present activity.

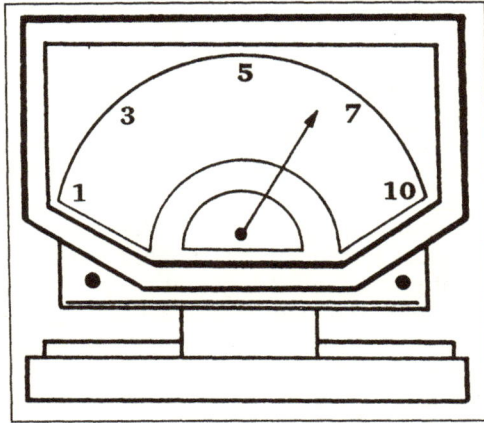

Figure 3: Human Energy Meter

If you discover continuous readings of 1-2-3 reevaluate your lifestyle. Your tiredness and inertia can probably be traced to a combination of poor diet, improper sleep, over work and lack of interest.

Perhaps you need to change your lifestyle. With gradual change your energy will improve.

> *Energy follows thought,*
> *There's where you're caught;*
> *Unconscious action,*
> *A scattered fraction.*
>
> *Energy follows thought,*
> *There's what you're taught;*
> *Consciously look,*
> *Read life's book.*
>
> *Energy follows thought,*
> *There's who you wrought;*
> *A being of light*
> *With cosmic sight.*
>
> *Light Wave 36*

Summary

1. We live in an energy universe. Every thing, person and event is a manifestation of energy vibrations.
2. To know what energy is, it must be consciously experienced.
3. Each will eventually learn to raise, lower or hold steady their energy level.
4. The body is not a thing, a lump of hard matter. The body is a dynamic master system of interrelated systems. The body is a dynamic configuration of energy units.
5. Still, you are not your body. More accurately, you are an energy being, a dynamic energy being in a dynamic energy world.
6. Recondition yourself to the life-fact: we live in an energy universe. When you touch something say, "This is a configuration of energy units."
7. Practice becoming an energy being until it is the only way you act, think, feel and speak.
8. Axiom I: Whatever it is you are going to do, there is just so much energy available to complete that action or complete a certain percentage of it.
9. Axiom II: If you go beyond that certain amount of energy for a specific length of time the activity inverts and a destructive use of energy results.
10. Test the two axioms. With application you will gradually become sensitive to the precise amount of time-energy (timergy) to complete an action or a percentage of it.
11. The First Law of Energy: Energy Follows Attention. Whatever you accomplish in this life it will demand your attention and energy.
12. Ask yourself, where do you place your attention each day? Use the 8-Spoked Wheel of Whole Living as a guide.
13. In order to consciously register and experience energy vibrations you must develop conscious sensitivity.
14. Practice the "vibing" exercise. What kind of energy-sensation do you pick up?
15. Note the positive and negative energies you register from others.
16. Using the Human Energy Meter as a mind-tool you can discover where you misuse energies and improve your energy use.

Chapter 8

The Science of Living

Whole Living

In order to become a truly whole, well-rounded person you must first see yourself from an overall viewpoint. If you practiced using the Eight-Spoked Wheel introduced in Chapter 7 (see figure 2 on page ?) you should have some idea where you are at.

Where do you channel your energies each day? What areas of the Eight-Spoked Wheel are not developed? By using the Wheel of Whole Living you will get an overview of yourself.

It may take a while to see yourself clearly. It's difficult for most of us to see ourselves. We tend to censor our "bad" points and even our "good" points depending upon the nature of our character.

Once you have a fairly clear overview of yourself you must see how the parts are inter-related and inter-dependent with one another.

Let's say you observe yourself in the area of social/relationships. Hardly a day goes by that you're not involved in some social activity. Now, if a high percentage of time-energy (timergy) is directed into the social then other areas are affected by being less developed.

Perhaps the spiritual and regenerative (self-rejuvenation) areas are left fallow. To live a full, whole life you must cultivate each area and inter-relate it to the other areas.

Perhaps you could widen your horizons by finding social activities where the spiritual and regenerative areas are tapped. Lectures, workshops, groups, classes, etc. might be a way of relating one area to another and thereby expanding your growth.

The first step in the Science of Living is to Know Yourself in True Proportion. The Greeks had this saying displayed over the portals to their mystery schools. A candidate for initiation was instantly rejected if he did not know himself. He had to know where he channeled his energies from day to day. He had to know what areas were more cultivated and those less cultivated.

Tuning to the Spiritual Frequencies at regular conscious intervals demands well-rounded, whole living. Just as a wheel with broken spokes breaks from the load, so will a person stray from their true course if they are not living a well-rounded life.

Lightergy vibration,
Star-field gyration;
Higher mind tune,
White light noon.

Superconscious one,
Diamond light sun;
Cosmic connection,
Soul convection.

Intelligent source,
The limitless force;
Ubiquitious field,
Consciously revealed.

Light Wave 37

Consciously Adapting To What Is

Adaptability - knowing how and when to bend, yield and adjust to the present condition, is the second step in the Science of Living.

The prerequisite for adaptability is consciousness. Consciousness involves purposeful effort toward heightened awareness. Consciousness means sustaining awareness. Consciousness results in seeing "What Is".

What Is refers to the dynamic energy universe. Sensing, registering and knowing the source of vital life vibrations is to see What Is.

Learning to see What Is is not enough. It is possible to see the situation at hand but not adjust to it flexibly.

Why? Because we have false memories, fixed images of the past, emotional blocks, subconscious hang-ups which prevent us from doing the most sensible thing. Instead, we often automatically go haywire, like some electronic robot.

When you feel yourself gripped by obsessive tendencies you have found a block, a fixed memory from the past which will stop you from full adaptability in the present.

What can you do? Next time, the time after and the time after that, etc., you catch yourself in a fixation, slow down, stop, take a deep breath. Turn your attention away from the fixation. (Remember - Energy Follows Attention)

The first few times may be difficult but with sustained effort, sensible determination and heartfelt prayer the blocks will dissolve from lack of energy. Conscious adaptability will follow.

Your efforts in flexibility will strengthen you. As you discover a new fixation, uproot it and eliminate it, your powers of adaptability will increase. It will seem and be much easier to adjust to present conditions.

You will encounter less roadblocks. Things will open up naturally. You will stop fighting yourself so much. You will sense-feel your purpose, what they call in the Orient your dharma - your structured duty in this life. Each new step in life will be clear to you, and you will adapt naturally.

Rays of golden light,
Streaming through the night;
Bursts of conscious thought
In cosmic mind wrought.

Colored energy essence,
Rainbow presence,
Frequency fields,
Intelligence wields.

Radiant star splash,
From matter to ash;
Birth to death turns,
The fiery mind burns.

Light Wave 38

Living Each Day

Recently I read a story in the paper about a young woman who survived a 10,000-foot fall from an airplane. She was an accomplished skydiver with nearly a hundred jumps.

As she said, "I was used to my chute opening. I kept pulling and pulling; it just wouldn't open."

She tried pulling her reserve chute, nothing. She plummeted toward the ground at over 100 mph.

Friends and relatives watched in horror as she apparently hit the ground behind some trees. When they found her she had miraculously landed in a pond. She was alive.

They rushed her to the hospital where emergency surgery was performed on her spine. It was successful. Six months later she was totally healed.

The reporter asked her how it changed her life. She replied, "Everything is different now. I see the beauty in the world - the sun, the trees, the flowers - everything is full of life. I see the love in others and I love others more.

"Every day is precious. I live one day at a time. Before I worried too much about the future. I fretted away hours reliving the past. Thank God, I am alive."

Living each day, living in the now - how can we achieve this without having to face death and survive?

Try the following - slow down, look, see. Notice every little thing. You haven't seen everything. Everything changes from moment to moment.

Observe shapes, colors designs, places, people, etc. Let go of rigid attitudes like life is difficult, hard, a drudgery.

Practice being aware and new worlds will open to you. The mundane will take on life. Your daily routine will seem more exciting.

If you notice yourself worrying about the future or fretting about the past, you are not living in the present. Live in the present. Take care of today. Live a whole life each day and the future will unfold.

By living each day, when difficulties arise, you will know what to do and you'll have the means to overcome your problems.

Become as a little child. Work, play, laugh, frolic - see the wonders, the mysteries, the new. Enjoy the company of others. Then you too can say, "every day is precious. I live one day at a time."

> *Limitless sea of light*
> *With waves crystal bright;*
> *Transparent ocean,*
> *Invisible motion.*
>
> *Thoughts of flame,*
> *Forms without name,*
> *Flicker in time,*
> *A universal rhyme.*
>
> *Ancient archons,*
> *Eternally harkens;*
> *The songs of fire*
> *From the angelic choir.*
>
> *Light Wave 39*

Conscious Function

Try the following exercise. For the next five minutes stop reading, get up and go about your business. Do everything you normally do but do it in slow motion.

Remember, slow motion like you see on TV. Now give it a try.

What did you notice? Was it easy, difficult or somewhere in-between? Did you want to do everything fast? Were you able to keep it up for five minutes?

We all tend to act unconsciously, automatically. Doing the same tasks and functions day after day after day we become mechanical. We start rushing. We jump from one thing to the next hardly noticing what we're doing.

Our daily living becomes a string of predictable habits. Someone observing us for one week could accurately predict the next week's activities and be 90 - 95% accurate.

We get caught up in our mechanical actions and are swept up into a vortex of rush. Like the rabbit in Alice in Wonderland, we're late for a very important date.

What can you and I do? Practice functioning consciously. While making the morning coffee, make it consciously. While driving to work, drive consciously. While eating dinner, eat consciously.

When I say consciously I mean slow down, become more attentive and relax. If you catch yourself acting like a go-go-go machine, stop, take a full deep breath and become keenly aware.

Another obstacle to conscious function is tension. Notice the tension in the muscles as you act. Let go of those tensions. Release them. Stop clutching them for dear life.

Practice functioning consciously every day. Gradually, you will be conscious in all you do. Like riding a bicycle, it will become second nature to you.

A Tip: The resistance to conscious function is often particularly powerful first thing in the morning. Once you wake up be sure to bring yourself to attention. Observe, look, see, listen and function consciously.

Avoid walking around in a vague sleepy stupor. If you discover this is a real problem for you, practice self-remembering. Say to yourself, "I (say your name to yourself or outloud) am completely aware in the here-now. Repeat three times. Every few minutes repeat three times until you are more attentive.

With harmony of sound
Your consciousness surround;
Melodic symmetry,
Wisdom's geometry.

Transparent hue,
A cosmic view;
Your mind stands still
So knowledge can fill.

Stretched to the heights
Touch heavenly lights;
Your hands will mold
The body of gold.

Light Wave 40

Octave Functions

If you run into a life problem that persistently causes frustration, disappointment and conflict, an octave function may help you handle it.

Before going any further let's offer a referent for "octave function". An octave function is a scale (at least 8 functions) of structured-practical ways to handle and overcome a pesky life problem.

There are at least 8 functions because usually one function does not have the necessary force to solve an habitual life problem.

Also, 8 functions allows for variety. We tend to get bored or stale with one function, eventually tiring of applying it. At that point, the life problem can reassert itself without meeting any counter-force. Furthermore, the numerous functions occupy your attention-energy, constructively allowing less energy to be focused on the problem.

Let's take a specific example and construct an octave function. We have all encountered a person impossible to get along with. This can be especially trying in a job situation because you are obligated to be around them.

First, make a column of numbers as follows:

F(1)
F(2)
F(3)
F(4)
F(5)
F(6)
F(7)
F(8)
ETC.

Notice the etc. at the end. This symbolizes the possibility of many more functions which can be of benefit.

Secondly, you want to come up with practical, usable functions. Where do you get them from?

Use your common sense. Use your brain-power. Concentrate. You may come up with a few.

Go to the library and the bookstore. Search out any reading material that may offer some suggestions. Ask your librarian for help.

Make up your octave function and test each one. If it helps keep it. If it's ineffective drop it and find a replacement. It may take a while to come up with an effective, comfortable combination of functions but once you do, you will solve your problems or at least handle them with minimal frustration.

Here's an octave function for handling a difficult person. Remember, you are better off coming up with your own.

F(1) Practice understanding. (For that person to be so messed up, they probably have many personal problems).

F(2) Practice patience. (Don't let it get to you, rise above it).

F(3) When frustrated take slow, deep, rhythmic breaths.

F(4) Mind your own business - stay on an impersonal level with them.

F(5) Agree with them when possible even if you don't agree.

F(6) Give them an occasional compliment to disarm them.

F(7) Show them respect despite their antagonistic character; it may change their attitude toward you.

F(8) Don't take sides, gossip or stir up trouble toward them.

ETC.

The Balanced Life

The balanced life, simply put, is moderation in all things. When you conscientiously and consciously avoid excesses you experience equilibrium.

Now, one of the major stumbling blocks to balanced living is our likes and dislikes. The more intense the like or dislike the more unbalanced we are in that area of life.

Observe yourself over the next few days. What do you really like to the point of indulgence? What do you push away? What do you really hate? If you take this exercise-experiment to heart you have won half the battle. Recognizing your intense automatic likes and dislikes is the first giant step.

How do you handle the automatic likes-dislikes in order to live the balanced life? When you begin catching yourself being carried along the swooping vortex currents of like-dislike, be aware of it. Stop identifying with it so intensely. See it as not even happening to you.

Now comes the crucial step; turn your attention elsewhere, on to something which will hold your attention, your interest. Even in desperation, turn your attention away.

Sometimes, we have obsessive habits and fears. We try to overcome them without success. Perhaps you are fighting them too much. In that case you are intensifying the habit or fear.

Stop fighting it. Turn your attention away. (This is often easier said than done -- practice, practice).

Sometimes, you may have to call on the help of others, on the help of spiritual frequencies, divine forces. As the saying goes, "God helps those who help themselves." Your efforts coupled with higher force increases your chances of overcoming intense habits and fears.

Living the balanced life brings a powerful force of stability into your auric-field. The stability is dynamic, flexible and strengthening.

Thought is the force
From the infinite source
Which creates a life
Of happiness or strife.

Thought is the force
Which steers a course
Through ups and downs,
Those smiles and frowns.

Thought is the force
Either smooth or coarse,
Can lift the soul
Or bury in a hole.

Light Wave 41

Summary

1. Tuning to the Spiritual Frequencies at regular conscious intervals demands well-rounded, whole living.
2. Adaptability is knowing how and when to bend, yield and adjust to the present condition.
3. The prerequisite for adaptability is consciousness. Consciousness involves purposeful effort toward heightened awareness.
4. Sensing, registering and knowing the source of vital life vibrations is to see What Is.
5. Your efforts in flexibility will strengthen you. As you discover a new fixation, uproot it and eliminate it, your powers of adaptability will increase.
6. If you notice yourself worrying about the future or fretting about the past, you are not living in the present.
7. By living each day, when difficulties arise, you will know what to do, and you'll have the means to overcome your problems.

8. Practice functioning consciously every day. Gradually, you will be conscious in all you do. Like riding a bicycle, it will become second nature to you.

9. A Tip: The resistance to conscious function is often particularly powerful first thing in the morning. Once you wake up be sure to bring yourself to attention. Observe, look, see and listen.

10. An Octave Function is a scale (at least 8 functions) of structured, practical ways to handle and overcome a pesky life problem.

11. The balanced life is moderation in all things. When you conscientiously and consciously avoid excesses you experience equilibrium.

12. Living the balanced life brings a powerful force of stability into your auric-field. The stability is dynamic, flexible and strengthening.

Chapter 8

The Science of Breath

The Effects of Breathing

I have met and read of some who have studied and practiced the science of breathing for 7, 10, 12 and even 20 years. The following pages are intended to be a mini-primer on the science of breathing. If they spark your interest and awareness, they have accomplished their appointed task.

No doubt if you have taken high school biology you are aware of the respiratory system and the critical importance of the breathing process.

I would like to quote Egyptian Master, Hamid Bey:

> *"One's mental quality and physical condition are dependent upon oxygen, for it is oxygen which gives life to the cells. Thus, the greater the oxygen intake, the healthier the cells, for the blood cells, as agents which carry oxygen to every part of the physical body, have more food - oxygen - to leave as the blood stream makes its unceasing tour to every and all parts of the physical body."*

> *"When we inhale, we draw in cool air; when we exhale we expel warm air. When the blood reaches the lungs after passing through the body, it is warm because it has collected much carbon dioxide and carbon dioxide is heat. It is this carbonic acid gas which is needed to burn and thus reduce the dead cells of the body to ashes ready to be thrown off, not only through the lungs but also through the elimination organs."*

"It is the completeness or incompleteness of this process which makes for health of the body and mind or dullness of body and mind. If the process is incomplete, a person cannot think clearly, has that tired feeling, is very lackadaisical, and suffers from lowered vitality."

Become aware of your breathing. Is it deep and rhythmic, shallow and unrhythmic or somewhere in-between? Do you get out into the fresh air daily?

After surveying your lifestyle, you see that you spend most of your time indoors, in smoke-filled rooms or driving in air polluted traffic. You need to practice better lung hygiene. Fresh air, rhythmic breathing, proper diet and regular exercise are necessary to improve your breathing process.

Consciously spend some time outdoors taking in deep full breaths of fresh air.

Raise your vibration
To a spiritual station;
Hear the celestial sounds
Making their spiral rounds.

Guard your thought-emotion
Stop a negative notion;
See the lighted forms
Through emotional storms.

Train your attention,
Make no pretension;
Tune to the presence,
Awakens the essence.

Light Wave 42

The Smoking Habit

It was reported on the radio recently that two billion dollars will be spent advertising cigarettes in third-world countries. The people of those countries are just beginning to go through the Industrial/Technological Revolution.

The truth is, smoking is on the decline in the West. The educated peoples of the developed countries are aware of the lie, smoking is a disease breeder. Thus, the greedy are looking for ignorant souls who can be fooled.

Years ago there were those who said, "stop smoking", "don't smoke" for moralistic reasons. Their moral code excluded cigarette smoking on the grounds that it corrupted you; it led to a life of further sin and degradation.

Although in some cases this may be partly true, we mostly know better today. Everybody knows your health will tend to suffer if you smoke. Lung and heart disease are partly the result of the smoking habit.

Still, there is yet another reason not to smoke, a psycho-spiritual reason. Now, if tar and nicotine restrict full rhythmic breathing, proper oxygen levels will not go through the blood stream. As a result, the blood will not be cleansed properly and the brain will not have enough oxygen to work efficiently.

In turn, your psycho-spiritual functions like attention, emotional calm, higher tuning, concentration, peak energy levels, etc. will not be up to par.

In order to kick the smoking habit there must first be awareness and knowledge. Secondly, there must be a complete disgust with the habit. Thirdly, there must be a method applied persistently to overcome the habit.

Numerous methods are available. If your disgust is great enough, no doubt you will attract the best method for you to quit.

Once you stop, you will feel more alive. Your senses will grow more acute. You will have money for other things.

Prana: Carrier Of The Life Force

"Prana the Sanskrit word for positive force which permeates the etheric earth sphere, including every individualized system thereof, and constitutes the motivating force of all forms." Vitvan

Prana, the electric, vibrant life force, courses through your veins and permeates your auric-field. With each breath you take, prana enters your body, carried by the oxygen.

Prana is a super oxygen, the energy which feeds and vitalizes the etheric body. The etheric body is a subtle, refined vehicle which interpenetrates the physical body (physiological organism).

The prana nourishes and energizes the organs of the etheric body, the force centers or chakras. When your breathing is irregular, shallow and rapid the prana cannot flow to the etheric body in sufficient force. You are weakened. Your auric-field becomes penetrable.

As a result, unbalanced forces are set in motion. Disease may begin to stir within your physical vehicle. The quality of your work and relationships drops. You are not yourself.

Have you ever been by a waterfall, high in the mountains, near the ocean or in a pine forest and taken a deep, full breath? How did you feel? Was the air any different?

It is a scientific fact that all of these places have a greater oxygen output as measured in negative ions. Negative ions of oxygen, when we breathe them in, have a revitalizing effect. Positive ions of oxygen, in smoke and smog, have a draining effect on the nervous system.

Obviously, then, places where air is charged with negative ions have a greater content of pranic force. Where do people go to get away from it all? Answers: the mountains, the seashores, the falls and the forests. Instinctively, we know these places make us feel better. The prana life force revitalizes.

You do not have to take a trip to energize yourself with pranic force. In the next two sections I will give you simple breathing exercises which can be used in the quiet comfort of your own home.

Star flame awaken,
Sleep forsaken;
Pleroma of light,
No more night.

There's a natural way
From night to day;
The sun's first light
Transmutes the night.

Keep the flame burning,
Experience learning;
Consciously tune to light,
Stars fill the night.

Light Wave 43

The Rhythmic Breath

Many times the rhythmic breath has been a life saver for me. Riding home on the subway after a long energy-sapping day's work, I began slow rhythmic breathing. By the time I reached home, I felt halfway alive again.

Sometimes I have felt just fine, walked into a situation where there was a large group of people and suddenly felt drained. The negative atmosphere, from negative thought-emotion people, was offset by rhythmic breathing.

Other times, I just wanted to relax attentively while watching television, and I'd begin the rhythmic breath. Ten or fifteen minutes later my senses were sharper, my mind clearer, my body relaxed.

There are several methods of rhythmic breathing. Let's begin with the counting method:
1. Sit upright.
2. Let go of tensions, especially in neck, jaw, back.
3. Inhale through the nose slowly as you count 1-2-3-4.
4. Exhale through the nose slowly as you count 1-2-3-4.

At first, continue for 3-5 minutes. Gradually, work your way up to 10-15 minutes.

Next time you're out for a walk try the walk-counting method. In rhythm with steps:

1. Inhale to the count of 1-2-3-4-5-6.
2. Hold bated breath to the count of 1-2-3.
3. Exhale to the count of 1-2-3-4-5-6.
4. Hold bated breath to the count of 1-2-3.
5. Continue this process for a few minutes as you walk.

As you perfect this method you can increase the count as you wish.

Master Hamid Bey, the Egyptian adept who founded the Coptic Order in the United States, practiced another method of rhythmic breathing. Instead of consciously counting the breath he simply observed the present rhythm of the breath.

1. Bring your attention to the chest cavity/lungs.
2. Observe the expansion-contraction process.
3. Don't interfere by changing anything.
4. Calmly watch the natural breathing process.

> *Arms, legs, head,*
> *Body desires bread;*
> *Hands, feet, eyes,*
> *Brain believes lies.*
>
> *Love, hate, fear,*
> *Feelings are a mirror;*
> *Like, dislike, pain,*
> *Lost memories insane.*
>
> *Words, ideas, thought,*
> *In a mind web caught;*
> *Noise, delusion, reason,*
> *Thinking has its season.*
>
> *Light Wave 44*

The Full Breath

Once again let's quote Master Hamid Bey.

> *"My Master told me that he could prophesy the life span of an individual if he knew exactly the average time consumed for each breath. The less time consumed - the faster a person breathes - the shorter the life span will be.*

"The deeper a person breathes - the longer the time it takes for one breath - the longer the span of life will be. This is because the life span of anyone is regulated by the equivalent, not only of the quality of the intake of oxygen and pranic force, but also by the quantity so it is of utmost importance that concentrated attention be given to both the quality and quantity of oxygen intake."

This can be achieved by practicing and perfecting the Full Breath. Proceed as follows:

1. Sit upright, yet comfortably.
2. Be attentive.
3. Slowly begin inhaling gently through the nose.
4. Continue the inbreath steadily until.....
5. You feel the walls of your chest cavity expand fully and until...
6. You feel your shoulders lifting then...
7. Take in even more and then exhale slowly.
8. Continue for 3-5 minutes at first
9. Gradually increase the time.

Singers, divers, athletes and orators develop deep breathing as part of their daily activities. The rest of us must increase our lung capacity through conscious steady effort.

Call it what you will,
Words are nil;
Quiet tune-feel,
Energies are real.

Metaphysical speech,
Deluded screech;
Present life-force
Experience the source.

Idle thought still,
Steady the will;
Now feel presence,
Dynamic quiescence.

Light Wave 45

Breathing And Emotional Calm

Do you recall the last time you got emotionally upset? Were you angry, irritable, annoyed? Did you realize how suddenly, impulsively and automatically you reacted?

We have all lost or misplaced something. We think we know where we put it, but it is not there.

We start searching all the likely places. We can't find it. The heart beats faster; the blood pressure soars. We're getting emotional.

Rhythmic breathing can calm the storm. As you're looking, begin slow rhythmic breathing through the nose. It will keep your mind clear so you can recall where you placed it.

Next time you fall into a nasty or dark mood, try rhythmic breathing. With more oxygen to blood and brain you begin to feel better. Then you have a greater chance of seeing what to do to overcome your difficulty.

Emotional reactivity can cause major problems in relationships. Attitudes, experiences and memories vary from person to person. Often the differences come to odds. Conflicts spark.

Angry, hostile words burst into full-blown arguments. Catch yourself being swept unconsciously into an angry emotional vortex. Begin rhythmic breathing. You can not be upset and breath rhythmically at the same time.

If you work with the public you know, hardly a day goes by without some hostile customer or client throwing the verbal one-two. You need your job in order to survive. You want to swing back, but you must turn the other cheek. Begin rhythmic breathing. Keep it up until you calm down.

I know this works. I was working in a gourmet shop in Manhattan one Christmas. It seems a customer I was serving was disturbed about something. She took it out on me.

She went wild, attacking everything I did loudly and viciously. I reacted angrily but fortunately remembered to begin rhythmic breathing.

She was a hurricane. The calmer I remained the angrier she got. The verbal abuse was incredible. I stopped the breathing for a half second and felt the sucking force pulling me into an argument. I desperately continued the breathing. The storm passed. I went about my day enjoying it fully.

Summary

1. Spend time outdoors taking in deep, full breaths of fresh air.
2. There's a psycho-spiritual reason for not smoking. Functions like attention, emotional calm, higher tuning, concentration, peak energy levels, etc. will not be up to par.
3. In order to kick the smoking habit there must be: A) awareness and knowledge, B) a complete disgust with the habit and C) there must be a method applied persistently.
4. Prana, the electric, vibrant life force, courses through your veins and permeates your auric field.
5. Prana is a super-oxygen, the energy which feeds and vitalized the etheric body.
6. Places where air is charged with negative ions has a greater content of pranic force. These places include: the mountains, the seashores, the falls and the forests.
7. Rhythmic breathing can energize you with pranic force.

8. Here are three methods of rhythmic breathing which can be practiced: A) the counting method, B) the walking-counting method and C) the observing method.

9. By practicing the full breath we can increase the quantity and quality of oxygen intake and lengthen our life.

10. Next time you're emotionally upset try rhythmic breathing. With more oxygen to blood and brain, you begin to feel better. Then you have a greater chance of seeing what to do to overcome your difficulty.

Chapter 10

The Science of Relaxation

Why We Become Tense

Tensions arise for three reasons:
1. Hyperactivity
2. Pressure points of the past
3. Too many simultaneous problems.

When we run around doing one thing after another in rapid-fire succession, we are hyperactive. We are not in control of our activity. We rush. A vortex of compulsive, automatic, impulsive action carries us along like a leaf in a river rapid.

Our society promotes hyperactivity. Commercials, the excessive zeal for sports and youth worship push action, action, action. Often we have the feeling if we are not doing something there is something wrong.

We are conditioned to feel bored if we are not active every second. Also, while active, we don't have to think about the whys and wherefores. It's too heavy to face. We have lost our sense of rhythm between activity - rest/relaxation.

Number two on the list of tension givers is pressure points of the past. Let's say you're with a friend, your wife or husband or a close family member. They say something or do something that annoys you, even gets you angry. The automatic emotional trigger is the result of some past emotionally charged memory.

Every time pressure points of the past are triggered, tensions automatically follow. You frown, grimace or furrow your brow. The muscles in your face tighten. The muscles and nerves go through all kinds of changes. This happens in a few seconds and usually you are unaware of it.

At one time or another we all have been confronted with major and minor crises. Usually a rapid succession of difficulties and problems hit you. Nerve and muscle lockjaw sets in.

Mental confusion, emotional trauma and bodily tension overcome you. Without the ability to relax, get calm and quiet the mind, even more difficulties arise until you're totally wiped out or get sick.

If you have mastered the skill of relaxation then at least you can take conscious steps to overcome your difficulties and pass through the crisis period without damage to your health and well-being.

The psyche is a lens
Through which light bends;
Images distorted,
Emotions contorted.

Sex, desires, love
and thoughts above -
Past life attraction,
Light wave refraction.

Lift psychic force
To noetic-field source;
Conscious attention the key,
Turn it and you're free.

Light Wave 46

What Is Relaxation?

What do you do when you relax? Read a book, watch TV, read the newspaper, take a walk, etc. Although these activities may relax you to a certain degree, they do not accomplish true relaxation.

Others escape in more self-destructive ways relaxing by drinking or smoking dope. True relaxation is not achieved in either of these ways.

What, then, is true relaxation? First, true relaxation is becoming aware of tensions. You become aware of body-tensions by placing your attention on various parts of your body and sense-feel various parts of your body and sense-feel the degree of tightness.

Place your attention at the back of your neck. How does it feel? Next, place your attention on your jaw and then on other parts of the body as you choose. Notice any tightness? Just become aware of tensions.

Many times after particularly stressful periods, your body speaks loud and clear - tension. You feel tight everywhere.

True relaxation does not allow you to become overly tense. There is a continuous monitoring of tension levels. At regular intervals there is a scanning of tensions. You then let go of the tensions before they build up. In the next sections, we will present various relaxation methods.

True relaxation involves mental-physical release of tensions. The mind-body functions as one unit. Tensions in the mind are felt in the body and tensions in the body are felt in the mind.

Do you recall the last time you prepared for a written exam? You studied and crammed before the test. Mental strain - body tension.

Do you remember the last time you were on your feet all day working? Your legs and feet began to ache. You felt tensions in your back and arms. By the time the day was over your mind was not sharp. It felt the bodily tensions.

Remember - escape and entertainment are not forms of true relaxation. Naturally, they are enjoyable and often release a limited degree of tension. Still, ultimately true relaxation can be achieved only as we are continuously aware of mind-body tensions.

Sickness, death and pain,
The mentally insane;
Against the natural order,
Within hell's border.

Non-cooperation,
Causes separation,
From peace and light
And what's presently right.

Understand nature's way,
Follow its bright ray,
Illumines each turn,
From moment to moment learn.

Light Wave 47

Passive Relaxation

What is meant by "passive relaxation"? In this context passive implies steady conscious effort in a quiet comfortable atmosphere. It does not mean letting events happen to you haphazardly.

Choosing and maintaining a quiet-comfortable spot is not a matter of fact task. The keyword here is spot. If you have been practicing the energy exercise from Chapter 7, Becoming An Energy Being, you have discovered every spot has an energy.

Wherever you choose to relax, your energy will be charged on that spot. The ability to relax will be that much easier because of relaxing vibrations set up on your spot.

As you become more consciously sensitive to energies you will become aware when someone else has been in your spot. If possible, try to explain to those close to you the importance of keeping your spot for you.

Realistically, difficulties and problems arise. Your quiet-comfortable spot will be submitted to chaotic emotional forces.

In order to restore the atmosphere to peace, cut two or three onions in half and place them on and around your spot. Before long the cleansing power of the onions will clear the atmosphere of negative energies.

Passive relaxation requires that you either sit up straight and attentive or lie down while maintaining a focus. Some say it is not wise to lie down when relaxing because the mind tends to drift. Or, there's a greater tendency to forget relaxation and fall asleep.

In my opinion, both ways are useful. It all depends on your psycho-physical state. Let's say your leg and back muscles are tight as a drum. You may be better off lying down and relaxing than sitting up.

On the other hand, let's say your neck and shoulder muscles are tight yet you're not too tired. It may be more comfortable to sit up and relax.

Proper rhythmic breathing is a crucial part of relaxation. In the following sections two passive relaxation methods will be outlined. Rhythmic breathing contributes to the success of both.

Open your eyes,
See blinding lies;
Watch where you're going,
Awareness is knowing.

Truth has pattern,
A guiding lantern;
Energy is real,
Know its feel.

Conscious function
Stops compunction;
Death is strife,
Light is life.

Light Wave 48

Two Relaxation Methods

Lie flat on your back on the floor. The floor is preferable to a bed or couch since it has much more supportive strength required for this exercise to work properly.

Before we go further begin slow, gentle rhythmic breathing through the nose. Keep your attention just below the nostrils so that you can feel the sensation of air entering as you inhale and exiting as you exhale. Continue rhythmic breathing for a few minutes. It will help you begin the relaxing process.

Now, still lying flat on the floor, feel your whole body as a great monumental weight and then give the weight up to the floor as much as you possibly can.

If you have to, begin with one part of the body, say the left leg, and continue with each section until you have given up its great weight to the floor.

Next, you want to loosen and let go of the tensions in the neck. You can do this while still lying on the floor by slowly, ever so slowly, rolling the head from side to side, first to the left and then to the right. Repeat this five to ten times until you feel a definite loosening in the back of the neck.

The master key to achieving a relaxed state is keeping your attention sharp and clear. When your awareness locates a point and you feel the tension, your feeling-consciousness will penetrate to the core of the tension.

This requires considerable concentration because the tension usually puts up a strong resistance. It tends to want to cling to itself.

Be persistent; continue entering into the tension. Miraculously it will begin to dissolve and dissipate. You will feel free from excessive stress.

This master key should be applied to every relaxation technique.

In this exercise you want to bring your attention to each part of the body in turn. Do not try to make anything happen. Just observe the effects. Be sure to give enough time for each part to relax. You do not have to lie on the floor. A comfortable chair, couch or bed is fine.

Here is the suggested order to follow:

1. Head: Place your attention on the brains, the scalp and forehead, the eyes, the nose, the ears, the cheeks and cheekbones, the jaw muscles and jaw bones, the lips and chin.

2. Spine: Place your attention on the base of the brains and the spine in the neck, the spine between the shoulders, the spine between the ribs, the spine in the waist, the base of the spine.

3. Back: Place your attention on the back muscles of the neck, shoulders and shoulder blades, ribs, waist and hips.

4. Front: Place your attention on the side and front muscles of the chest, the side muscles of the waist, the muscles of the pit of the stomach, the muscles of the abdominal wall.

5. Functions: Place your attention on the nose and breathing, the tongue from root to tip, the gums and teeth, the roof of the mouth, saliva and the mouth watering, the swallow, the inside of the neck, the lungs (loose and open to circulation), breathing freely, the inside of the pit of the stomach, the region of the solar plexus, the whole of the inside of the abdominal regions (loose and open to circulation), heaving freely.

6. Arms: Place your attention on the shoulders and shoulder joints and muscles, the muscles between the shoulders and the elbows, the elbows, the forearm muscles, the wrists, the palms of the hands, the backs of the hands, the knuckles, the finger joints, the nails, the fingertips.
7. Legs: Place your attention on the hip joints and hip muscles, the thigh muscles, front and back, the knee caps, the knee joints the backs of the knees, the shins down to the ankles, the calves and tendons of achilles down to the heels, the ankles, the insteps, the balls of the feet, the toes down to the nails, the soles of the feet.

This exercise may seem difficult at first. If you get tired, stop. Build gradually to the point where you can go through all the steps. With practice you will be able to complete the exercise in just a few minutes.

It is worth mentioning that both of these techniques are excellent if you have a problem going to sleep at night.

> *Psychic energy raise*
> *From the maya maze*
> *To the noetic field,*
> *The light being shield.*
>
> *Let go automatic thought*
> *Most thinking is for naught;*
> *Redirect psychic urge*
> *So light can resurge.*
>
> *In emotion's mighty hold*
> *Transmute heat to cold,*
> *Channel the raging fire*
> *Up thru the crown's spire.*
>
> *Light Wave 49*

Relaxation Circuits

Sometimes, when your energy level is so low that you just don't have the concentration to relax, it's wonderful to have a relaxation circuit. A relaxation circuit is a device or tool that increases your energy level and helps you become more relaxed.

The Eeman relaxation circuit (see figure #4 on page 84) is a godsend, especially when tired, drained, and/or exhausted. The Englishman L.E. Eeman discovered that by using copper screens and wires connected in natural body circuits, tensions can be released.

Specifically, you lie down with one copper screen behind the head (positive pole). You run a wire from the head screen to your left hand (negative pole). Run the wire to the right hand for lefties.

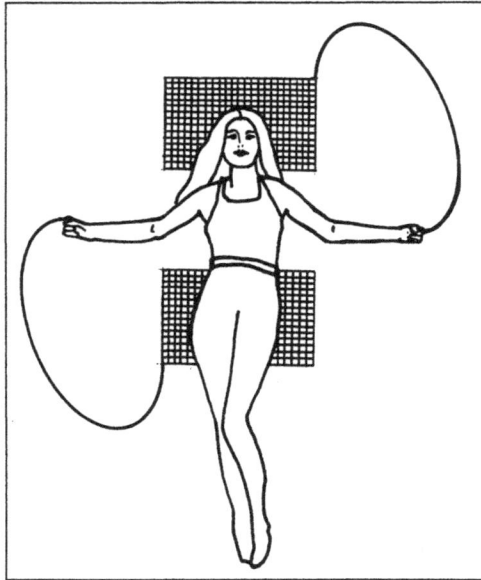

Figure 4: Eeman Relaxation Circuit

Next, you place the other copper screen at the base of the spine (negative pole). Run another wire from this screen to your right hand (positive pole).

For optimum relaxation run a third wire between the two screens. Then, lie comfortably for about 20-30 minutes. Be sure to cross your legs at the ankles to enhance circulation.

Relaxation circuits are excellent for detuning and detaching you from negative rapports. A negative rapport is a sympathetic vibration registered/felt from a person, place, or thing which is not harmonious to your energies.

Negative rapports can manifest as negative emotions like anger, fear, guilt, and depression. They can also manifest as physical sensations like tension headaches, stabbing in the stomach and a heavy heart.

At the onset of a negative rapport, use a relaxation circuit as soon as possible. Much of the negative will be released within 10-20 minutes.

To learn more about relaxation circuits or to order, write Life Energy Sciences. The address for Life Energy Sciences is in the back of this book.

Tuning to the Spiritual Frequencies

Beings of light,
Conscious sight,
Balanced will,
Thought waves still.

Beings of light,
Minds of might;
Guiding stars,
Healing scars.

Beings of light,
Wisdom's right;
Love's release,
Knowing peace.

Light Wave 50

Active Relaxation

Active relaxation means using the least amount of energy necessary to do a particular task. If we learn to work without unnecessary tensions, we would not be so tired out at the end of the day.

Here are two active relaxation techniques:

1. Sitting Exercise:

    Those who spend a good part of the day sitting, such as secretaries, receptionists, accountants, artists, etc. need to "sit back and relax". The first step is letting the chair hold you. In other words, give your whole weight up to the chair. Let it hold you up.

    At first it takes sustained concentration. Sit back and relax on and off throughout the day. Whenever you catch yourself grabbing onto yourself (tensing) give yourself up to the chair again.

2. Standing Exercise:

    Many daily activities demand that you stand on your feet for many hours on end. These include cops, sales people, cashiers, etc. Naturally, you need to wear comfortable shoes, but there are other steps you can take.

    As much as possible give the entire weight of your body over to the floor or ground. Let the ground or floor hold you up. In this way you will not inwardly grab the muscles of your legs in an unnatural attempt to hold yourself up.

    Another tip is to feel your legs heavy. Imagine each leg weighing a thousand pounds. This technique is also helpful for those who do a lot of lifting. It has a way of getting the energies to a lower center of gravity so the lift works upward.

Learning to relax throughout the day increases your powers of perception, your ability to relate with others and the enhancement of your creative talents.

Summary

1. Tensions arise because of: a) hyperactivity, b) pressure points of the past and c) too many problems.
2. True relaxation is becoming aware of tensions.
3. True relaxation does not allow you to become overly tense. There is a continuous monitoring of tension levels. You let go of the tensions before they build up.
4. True relaxation involves mental-physical release of tensions.
5. Tensions in the mind are felt in the body and tensions in the body are felt in the mind.
6. Passive relaxation involves steady conscious effort in a quiet-comfortable atmosphere.
7. Wherever you choose to relax, your energy will be charged on that spot. The ability to relax will be that much easier because of relaxing vibrations set up on your spot.
8. Proper rhythmic breathing is a crucial part of relaxation. Rhythmic breathing contributes to the success of relaxation exercises.
9. The master key to achieving a relaxed state is keeping your attention sharp and clear.
10. When your awareness locates a tension point and you feel the tension, your feeling-consciousness will penetrate to the core of the tension.
11. A relaxation circuit is a device or tool that increases your energy level and helps you become more relaxed.
12. L.E. Eeman discovered that using copper screens and wires connected in natural body circuits can release tensions.
13. Active relaxation means using the least amount of energy necessary to do a particular task.
14. Learning to relax increases your powers of perception and your ability to relate harmoniously with others.

Chapter 11

The Science of Semantics

What Is Semantics?

The word semantics is most often used in the popular sense to mean a different way of putting the same thing. On television talk shows, in the newspaper and in everyday conversation people disagree. Rather than get to the bottom of their disagreement, they may say something like "It's semantics", "It's just a matter of semantics".

This use of the word semantics, though perhaps valid and useful in its own right, has very little to do with the science of semantics.

The science of semantics is the study of how words effect us mentally, emotionally and physically.

In order to understand how words influence our psychological nature, we must be aware of what's known as the "semantic reaction".

Have you ever watched a television commercial about a favorite food, perhaps a particularly tasty, scrumptious, mouth-watering candy bar? After listening to the commercial you had to have one, in fact, you were compelled to immediately go to the store. You have had a dramatic semantic reaction.

The first practical step for the student of semantics is to observe semantic reactions in oneself, in others and in the world at large. Become acutely aware of what words trigger you to destructive, constructive and moderate behavior.

Do words of praise motivate you to achieve? Does criticism cripple you? Are you elated by positive sounding words even when there are no actual events behind it? Are you thoroughly depressed by verbal attacks against you even when you know they are not true?

Knowing and applying the science of semantics to your life is a must if Tuning to the Spiritual Frequencies is to be a consistent reality. If you are constantly and automatically identifying with words passing through your mental sphere the spiritual frequencies cannot vibrate on/in/through your aura effectively.

When you begin to control your semantic reactions (s.r.) then the old saying, "sticks and stones can break my bones but words can never hurt me" rings true.

You and I are the value givers. If you identify, give value, assign meaning to words used, then *you* have done so. It is your responsibility not the other fellow's. Words in and of themselves are essentially meaningless. You give them shades of meaning, degrees of power over your psyche by your semantic reactions.

Images in the mind
Will make you blind,
To energy-light
And functional right.

Words are noise,
Intellectual toys;
Light-energy is real,
Experience its feel.

Consciously abstract,
Notice how you react;
Stop image-word flow,
Let the light glow.

Light Wave 51

The Word Is Not The Thing

There is a clear and undisputed fact regarding the realm of words; in this world *the word is not the thing.*

You can not drive the word *car*; you cannot eat the word *hamburger*; you cannot smell the word *flower*.

Unless a word has a referent in structural reality (in the energy world) it is meaningless; it is nothing but a nonsense noise.

No one disputes the definite fact that the word is not the thing yet most use words everyday as if they have meaning when they don't.

For example, have you ever overheard a couple arguing about something that hasn't happened yet.

"I don't want to go to the Johnson's party; I don't have the dress I need."

"We've got to go; it's good for business."

The party has not occurred; it is not a reality. People can go on and on about something that has never happened.

Here's an example. It's night in your house or apartment. You wake up, get out of bed and go into the other room. The shade moves. You believe someone is there.

Your body reacts to the belief "someone" is there. Your heart beats faster. You feel fight-flight. Then you realize it was only the wind.

The word "someone" had no meaning in structural reality. You gave it a temporary false reality which you reacted to as if it were real.

Nothing particularly harmful came out of these misuses of words. Still, there are incidents which may result in tragedies. Governments use nonsense lie-words, propaganda, to stir and steer public opinion. The words have no basis in fact but the power hungry leaders have manipulated opinion to their desired ends. This false use of words has senselessly been the catalyst for war or the prolongation of death and destruction.

An excellent analogy clarifying the point further is, "the map is not the territory."

Let's say you want to travel from Washington, D.C. to Boston by car. The map shows Philadelphia as the main city along the way. If you follow that map you waste time, gas and energy.

If you follow another map that has New York City between Washington, D.C. and Boston your map reflects the territory more accurately and will save you time, gas and energy.

Still, the map is not the territory; the word is not the thing. If the map or the word refers and reflects structural reality accurately then it has a degree of usefulness and, therefore, meaning. If they have no basis in structural reality then they are meaningless yet possibly dangerous.

> *Lift psychic force;*
> *Change its course,*
> *Upward to the field,*
> *Spirit's shining shield.*
>
> *Raise desire's heat*
> *Beyond the heart's beat,*
> *Beyond the head's chatter*
> *Till on the cosmic ladder.*
>
> *Let go emotion's hold,*
> *Transmute to noetic gold;*
> *Transform thought jolt*
> *Into a light wave bolt.*
>
> Light Wave 52

Consciousness Of Abstracting

Tuning to the Spiritual Frequencies demands the skill of consciously abstracting. Second by second, minute by minute, hour by hour we abstract; we draw data through the five sensory channels.

You must become more aware of what you are abstracting - the sound, the color, the form, the texture, the taste, the smell, etc. Become more attentive of the abstracting process.

When we are unconscious of the abstracting process there's a powerful tendency to become fixed, rigid, habit-bound. The possibility of Tuning to the subtle Spiritual Frequencies is temporarily eclipsed.

Images and words then take on false meanings. We believe they are real. Only energy is real. Images and words were only meant to be maps, signs and symbols referring to the energy reality.

Instead, when we are unconscious of the abstracting process we lose touch with the present-now, the non-verbal, non-image level and give inappropriate value to the words and images. Ultimately, we identify so intensely with the false reality of words and images that we unconsciously forfeit our spiritual tuning.

How can you stop identifying with the false word-image world? There are many functional techniques that may prove useful to you individually. I will present three. Test each thoroughly. What result do you get? Do you feel and abstract differently?

First, choose an object, any object; for example, a pen. Now, I want you to write down everything you can about the pen. Be sure to write down everything about the pen.

Once you've completed your list and you feel you have written down everything, try hard to think of just one more. Fine. Are you satisfied you've said everything? You are?

Have you described the chemical and molecular structure of the pen? Have you listed the atomic structure? Do you get the point?

In reality, you can never know everything about the pen. The pen is a non-verbal energy pattern vibrating in a ·continual dance of change. Literally, from second to second the pen is different, although unnoticed by the physical senses.

A brand new pen is not exactly like a pen five years old. There are obvious differences. Shrink the time frame to one-tenth of a second; there are not so obvious differences. Just because your eyes cannot see them doesn't mean it's not so.

The second exercise tests your consciousness to become more aware of the orders of abstracting. Whatever you perceive on the sensory level is abstracting from energy structures.

Let's use the pen once again. The atoms, molecules and chemicals composing the microscopic structure of the pen are vibrations of energy. You can tune to and sense the vibratory field of the pen. That's the non-verbal level which I'll refer to again in exercise three.

For now I want you to become aware of the existence of the non-verbal energy level. Next, I want you to become aware that you abstract an image in your mind of the pen. After that, you give that abstracted image a name. That's a "pen".

Practice noticing this process: 1) non-verbal level, 2) image in the mind and 3) name-word. Catch yourself forming an image. Watch how automatically you assign words to the image.

The final exercise requires sustained concentration. Practice silence on the non-verbal level. Stop identifying with images and words in the mental body. Tune to the energy world.

The more you practice this exercise the more conscious you will become of the energy-reality. Then you more easily Tune to the Spiritual Frequencies.

> *Images in the mind*
> *To delusions bind;*
> *Pictures of things*
> *Have invisible strings.*
>
> *Feel the energies real,*
> *Stop the mental wheel;*
> *Tune to wisdom's way,*
> *Dawn of a new day.*
>
> *Mental movie illusion*
> *Breeds daily confusion;*
> *Experience light waves,*
> *Leave the mind caves.*
>
> *Light Wave 53*

The Only Content Of Knowledge Is Structure

The ability to know anything directly requires the skill of direct experiencing. In order to experience directly you must practice silence on the non-verbal level.

Once you have stopped the word-noise, the mental-emotional chatter of the psyche you are on the verge of knowing directly from experience.

Approaching the structure of reality from energy, vibration, forces, fields, frequencies and then registering these dynamic modulations through perceptive faculties means the end of mere information and the beginning of true knowledge.

You go to school; you memorize the state capitals, you gather, store and regurgitate an endless chain of facts about this and that.

The question is -- what do you know? Unless you have a direct experience of any person, place or thing you do not know a thing! You may "think you know" but that is not the same as knowing directly.

Registering the energy is an experience. Have you ever gone into a public place, say a business, and felt "negative vibes"? If you have any degree of awareness whatsoever, you have had such an experience.

At that moment you know that atmosphere. The field of energy at that particular moment is negative or destructive. Often you experience it physically as a drained feeling or sudden tiredness. You know because you are experiencing the structural reality of that immediate environment.

Now, if somebody else told you about the "negative vibes" in that place, the verbal information they have passed on to you on the mental level is not knowing.

Why is this distinction so important when Tuning to the Spiritual Frequencies? Because as you grow spiritually, evolve and manifest your true structure, function and order in this life, you must differentiate knowledge from information. If you hear about or read about the importance of concentration, get excited about the possibility and then identify, believe you have superior powers of concentration, you have blocked your growth.

Blocking natural growth, in effect, detunes you to a greater or lesser degree to the spiritual frequencies. On the other hand, if you differentiate information from knowledge, you open the door to experiencing the skill of concentration.

What you actually know and what you know *about* are vastly different. Review your store of knowledge. How much do you know from experience?

When you speak are you speaking from your direct experience or from what you've read, heard of or been told about?

By recognizing the difference and moving toward experiencing the energies and vibrations of reality more immediately, you have access to knowledge and you will experience the difference for yourself.

Consciousness is clear,
Reflections in a mirror;
Emotionally detached,
Structurally matched.

Consciousness is steady,
Eternally ready,
Observing motion
Beyond notion.

Consciousness is power.
Transforms the hour
From psychic mire
To noetic fire.

Light Wave 54

Words Are Multiordinal

In the science of semantics there's a root premise indicated by the word multiordinal. All words are multiordinal; they have no meaning in and of themselves. A word has meaning only when used in a particular context. The same sounding word has a different shade of meaning in another context.

For instance, if someone used the phrase, "she's red," what does it mean? It means nothing; it is a word-noise. Give it no value.

Now, if you knew the context, the life situation the phrase "she's red" takes on meaning.

She's red...
1. blushing from embarrassment
2. with rage
3. from a sunburn
4. having cut herself
5. where she burned her finger
6. head to toe wearing an all red outfit
7. every word (if you didn't know the spelling)
8. all of his books
9. etc.

You could go on and on and on with this list of contexts. Even the contexts used have a wide range of various meanings. There are degrees of red when sunburned — a mild burn to a severe burn.

Why is it important to realize words are multiordinal? On an everyday level we converse back and forth in business, in friendships, in families, etc. Most conflicts in relationships stem from fixing a meaning for a word and then believing everyone else should have the same meaning for that same word.

Let's say there are two friends who like to ski. They drive to the ski area. One skier is a beginner, the other is an intermediate. The beginner says, "it's great to be up in the mountains." The intermediate skier reacts by saying, "Up? What do you mean? We're not up in the mountains until we take the chairlift to the top." Now the beginner skier, not knowing semantics, could have a semantic reaction, like the intermediate skier did, and take his friend's statement as personal criticism. Then you'd have the basis for personal conflict.

The word "up" is multiordinal and has meaning relative to a point of reference. An airline pilot might tell the intermediate skier, "you haven't been "up" until you've flown at 35,000 feet, higher than any mountain." In turn, an astronaut might tell the airline pilot, "there's no up or down; there's only space."

On an international level the multiordinality of words becomes critical. Taking words in rigid ways and not being sensitive to contexts and shades of meaning can lead to struggles, wars and the death of thousands and even millions.

When Tuning to the Spiritual Frequencies keep the multiordinality of words in mind. Getting fixated, rigidly identified with a particular word and your personal meaning for it, can set up a static in the psyche blocking the natural flow of higher energies into your individual field.

The next section will indicate how to avoid and eliminate automatic, fixed semantic reactions.

Centered in the field,
Apocalypse unsealed;
Feel noetic mind
Love frequencies kind.

Tune-feel wisdom's way,
Higher vibrations ray;
Structured will awake,
An ordered life make.

Understanding's energy feel,
Tempered strength of steel;
Conquer elemental desire,
Hear the heavenly choir.

Light Wave 55

The Thalamal-Cortical Gap

When you automatically identify with anything, you are operating from the thalamus level. The thalamus is located at the base of the brain and is the reactionary center.

When you consciously abstract and are centered in the infinite valued orientation you tend to register - pause - then react, act, do nothing -- in short, choose.

The pause is known as the thalamal-cortical gap. Being conscious is being centered in the cortex at the front of the brain. When conscious of abstracting, the cortical functions are active, shortcircuiting the impulse reactions of the thalamus.

In order to develop the thalamal-cortical gap and, as a result, handle life situations more effectively, you must become aware of the "is" of identity. Automatic identifications are often triggered by the word "is".

For instance, "Tim is a good boy", "Bill is a doctor", and "Laura is a negative person".

If you are consciously abstracting, you will pause when hearing each of the previous statements. You will know the statement "Tim is a good boy" is meaningless, a noise. Without a context, an experience and a referent for the word good, "Tim is a good boy" has no meaning.

Now, if you are not conscious of abstracting you may very well automatically attribute meaning to the statement "Tim is a good boy". Then the false imagination hooked to past associative memories may go haywire with meaningless identifications.

You may assume all kinds of actions that to you are "good" about Tim. He eats all his vegetables, works hard in school and goes to bed on time. These assigned attributes may have nothing to do with the real Tim, the non-verbal activities of Tim on the energy level.

This tendency to give meaning where there is no meaning can get you into trouble. In some instances, it may be a matter of survival.

Let's say you're driving on a mountain highway. There are many curves all appropriately indicated by road signs. You begin to assume that if you follow the signs you'll be prepared for every curve.

With that identification you stop consciously abstracting. You stop functioning from the cortex with the conscious sense, the thalamal-cortical gap. The flexibility and adaptability of rapid choice survival action is reduced if not altogether eliminated.

Let's say the next curve is not marked. Perhaps the sign blew down. You are not paying attention.

Suddenly the curve is upon you. You are not functioning consciously so you react from the thalamus. If your instincts are sharp, you'll make the turn. If your instincts react with fear, you may not survive. An accident, injury or even death may result.

Awareness creates a pause that allows for a variety of choices. One Tuning to the Spiritual Frequencies must navigate the vortexes of life by being conscious. There are force-fields of negativity that can be easily avoided by being aware. The pause, the thalamal-cortical gap, allows for flexibility in handling whatever situation is at hand.

Summary

1. The science of semantics is the study of how words affect us mentally, emotionally and physically.
2. The first practical step for the student of semantics is to observe semantic reactions.
3. If you are constantly and automatically identifying with words passing through your mental sphere, the Spiritual Frequencies cannot vibrate in your aura effectively.
4. Words in and of themselves are essentially meaningless. You give them shades of meaning, degrees of power over your psyche by your semantic reactions.

5. The word is not the thing. You cannot drive the word car; you cannot eat the word hamburger; you cannot smell the word flower.

6. The false use of words can be the senseless catalyst for war or the prolongation of death and destruction.

7. If the word refers and reflects structural reality accurately then it has a degree of usefulness and, therefore, meaning.

8. Tuning to the Spiritual Frequencies demands the skill of consciously abstracting.

9. When we are unconscious of the abstracting process, there's a powerful tendency to become fixed, rigid, habit-bound.

10. We can identify so intensely with the false reality of words and images that we unconsciously forfeit our Spiritual Tuning.

11. Practice noticing this process: 1) non-verbal energy level, 2) image in the mind and 3) name-word.

12. Practice silence in the non-verbal level. Stop identifying with images and words in the mental body. Tune to the energy world.

13. Approaching the structure of reality from energy, vibration, forces, fields, frequencies and then registering these dynamic modulations through perceptive faculties means the end of mere information and the beginning of true knowledge.

14. Registering energy is experience.

15. All words are multiordinal. They have no meaning in and of themselves. A word has meaning only when used in a particular context.

16. Most conflicts stem from fixing a meaning for a word and then believing everyone else should have the same meaning for that word.

17. When you consciously abstract and are centered in the infinite-valued orientation you tend to register - pause - (thalamal-cortical gap) then act, react, do nothing; in short, choose.

Chapter 12

The Sci-Art of Love

What Is Love?

Love is a vibration. Love is not words or thoughts. Love is a frequency band of energies that can be felt and expressed.

To help you remember that love is an energy I'm going to introduce the word "Lovergy". When you experience a love vibration it is lovergy.

When you hug a friend, family member, wife, husband or romantic partner lovergy flows. Lovergy is felt as a flow of energy between two people. Often there are feelings of warmth, happiness, contentment, joy, etc. accompanying the lovergy.

Lovergy has an integrative affect on our mind-psyche-body. In fact, lovergy binds us together. Without lovergy there would be no marriage, no children, no family, no society, no country, no human race.

Love bonds us together. The hate vibration pulls us apart. What happens to a person with little or no love in their life? Self-destructive and other destructive behavior is prominent. They do not eat properly, sleep properly, think clearly or act harmoniously.

When you feel scattered, upset, distraught, when thought, emotion, desire and action are pulling in different directions, what pulls you back together? Lovergy brings the pieces back together.

You talk it out with a best friend over lunch. Someone who loves you tells you it's okay, everything will work out. They love you; they understand.

The renowned psychologist Carl Jung visited the Taos Indians. He asked their chief what he thought about world conditions.

The chief answered first by clarifying two different kinds of thought. "The white man thinks with his head; we think with our hearts."

He went on to say. "Someday soon the sun will go out if more people do not think with their heart. By thinking with his head the white man is destroying the earth, the sky, the water . . ."

Each must think-feel more with the heart in order to experience lovergy. Hug those you love. Tell them you love them. Show intelligent kindness and consideration to others. Love your body, the temple of the soul, and take care of it.

Love yourself; accept who you are.

These few simple actions on a daily basis will get you thinking more with your heart. Your immediate, direct and ongoing experience of the love force will tell you what love is better than any explanation in print.

As long as you resent, hate, seek revenge and harbor hostility, you disrupt your life, push away the healing force of love and beat a path to self-destruction.

No matter how upset or antagonistic you might feel, tune into lovergy. Hold your attention on love. Love the sky, the water, the trees and the earth. Love everything and everyone. When you're experiencing the love vibration it is difficult to hate.

Believing images are real
Chains you to the wheel
Of birth and death,
Of first and last breath.

Light-energy feel
Breaks the hermetic seal;
Opens the frequency world
Spiral growth uncurled.

Sensory sight is slow
Cannot see the glow;
Pictures feed delusion,
Light dissolves illusion.

Light Wave 56

Roadblocks To Love

Love is not only a vibration, a frequency of energy, it is also the unifying, synthesizing force in the cosmos. From galaxy to planet, from sky to sea, from elephant to ant, love is the unifying force.

In other words, love is everywhere, in everything. That being true, why isn't there more love flowing and circulating between the peoples of earth? Because there are roadblocks to love.

Some of the roadblocks to love include hatred, resentment, anger, pride... a host of self-centered emotions. It is amazing, even mind-boggling, to know that love is everywhere yet so many have so much difficulty and frustration maintaining loving relationships.

Our preconceived ideas about love are awesome roadblocks. When we imagine love to be a certain way before the actual experience, love cannot be felt fully in the moment. The fantasy of love is never the reality of love.

The fantasy-reality conflict disturbs, disrupts and destroys the current of love energy flowing between husbands/wives, friends, siblings, lovers, countries, etc.

Love is a *NOW* force. You need to drop your fantasies, imaginings, hopes, fears and past pain. When you are here in the present with another, lovergy can be felt almost instantaneously. The roadblocks are removed.

Putting limits on love will also reduce its flow. Some people falsely believe that love can only be experienced in romance. If they have not fallen in love then they search desperately for romantic excitement.

To limit love in this way is to cut yourself off from love's ubiquitous experience. Watch a sunset, see a boy playing with his dog, notice a mother hugging her baby, listen to some beautiful music . . . the world is teeming with love.

Once you become aware that love is literally everywhere, you want to express that love. You want to serve others not just make money. You want to give what you can, not just take all you can get.

Have you ever heard yourself or someone say, "I'm afraid I'll get hurt"? Fear: another roadblock to love. An ancient poet wrote, "It is better to have loved and been hurt than never loved at all."

The fear of being hurt dams up the loving, giving, sharing and caring which you naturally feel with another. Sure you might get hurt along the way. So what! Feel hurt, then go on. The joy of loving is far more fulfilling than the agony of the hurt.

The law of the opposites comes into play here. If you know someone who holds back from love because of the fear of being hurt, what do you notice? The fear of love/attract love cycle creates a conflict of the opposites.

These people push away love intensely then attract love intensely. After a while they become crushed by the love-hurt conflict. It's either feast or famine.

Once a person stops identifying with the hurt, they just love. Love knows when to give more, less or not at all. The person who thinks with their heart has removed the roadblocks to love.

Tune-feel-know
Everything aglow;
Matter is alive
As a beehive.

Feel divine presence
Everything is essence;
Physical is energy,
Vibrating spacergy.

Feel noetic force
Every cell's resource;
Body is dynamic
Energy quick.

Light Wave 57

Conscious Love

Relationships release energy. What do you feel when you spend time with someone you are attracted to? You don't feel drained, right? Instead you feel new life, greater vitality, energized.

Currents of love begin to flow, vibrate and permeate your psyche. You think a lot about this wonderful new person. You want to be with them. You can't wait to see them again because it feels so good.

This great energy release is not necessarily the love of your life. It may be a temporary exchange of life energy. Each may offer an energy that the other is seeking.

Conscious love is aware. It knows not to take this great burst personally. Conscious love takes it more impersonally. The initial energy exchange is thoroughly enjoyed but not reduced to personal, romantic or sexual love.

Someone who is striving to Tune more to the Spiritual Frequencies must clearly discriminate the difference between personal, possessive love and impersonal, unconditional love.

As you become more sensitive to energies, vibrations and frequencies, you will feel the energies released in relationships more intensely. If you take this release personally you will be carried from one affair to another.

If this occurs you will go unconscious. When you are unconscious, you cannot Tune to the Spiritual Frequencies. Conscious love takes the initial burst of relating energies impersonally. As a result, the joy of a revitalizing energy exchange is not reduced to a temporary affair. Instead, the possibility of a lasting friendship is presented.

Unless there is spiritual and mental compatibility as well as emotional and physical compatibility, there is little if any chance the relationsip will last more than a few months.

On a recent television comedy show the woman character is attracted to a younger, muscular hunk. She decides to go out with him. After the date she comments to her mother, "It was great as long as he didn't talk".

Physical attraction, the release/exchange of energy on the physical level, is the most short-lived attraction. Without common likes and dislikes, clear communications and shared spiritual beliefs, the relationship tends to fade away.

Sooner or later the initial excitement, the irresistable attraction disappears. Often at the end of superficial relationships there's disappointment, disgust, hostility and anger.

Conscious love knows that after the beginning flash which blinds, another phase of energy excitement begins. If there is more than just physical attraction then communication expands and spiritual views are exchanged.

I have met couples who have little if any awareness of the partner's spiritual convictions or lack thereof. I recently had a counseling session with a woman who was about to get married. She didn't even know her fiance's religious background.

> *Transform negative traits,*
> *Automatic loves and hates;*
> *Into positive force,*
> *Refining toward the source.*
>
> *Touch and let go*
> *The psychic low;*
> *Transmute the lead*
> *To golden bread.*
>
> *Digest the stale past,*
> *Remove the memory cast;*
> *From purification*
> *To regeneration.*
>
> *Light Wave 58*

Touching, Hugging, Holding Hands

The interchange of lovergy is most immediate when touching, hugging or holding hands. If there is little or no touching, hugging or holding hands in your everyday life then love has ceased to flow through you to others and back again.

The heartfelt thrill and excitement of hugging a baby or small child is one of the purest exchanges of love. The child gladly and earnestly receives your affections. There is no resistance. The child bathes in love's glowing and uplifting force.

As the years go on and the child experiences anger, hostility and violence to its being, then he or she begins to show signs of resisting the love currents. The child imitates adult behavior. He or she sees what adults cruelly do to each other. The natural inclination to hug subsides. Afterall, mommy and daddy don't hug.

Tuning to the Spiritual Frequencies requires an evaluation of loving touch. The inner life manifests love through service, giving and the gentle caring touch.

Is there romance without caresses? Can there be friendship without touch? Can there be love of a child without hugging?

Invisible currents of love energy flow with caring touch. Subtle connections between inner love feelings and the people you love are established with a touch.

Loving bonds melt away the illusion of self-separateness, isolation and loneliness. In truth, we are all interconnected. The false personality, the selfish ego, imagines it can survive without tender loving touch.

Everyone knows or has met an antagonistic person. Do you ever see them touch? An angry person touches violently. They hit, scratch, bite, kick, punch, etc. They resist touching, hugging and holding hands.

Everyone knows or has met a loving person. At every opportunity they touch. They naturally want to show their affection. Their heart overflows with love, especially for those close to them like friends, family, husband, wife, lover.

Toward which end of the spectrum do you fall? Do you avoid love and the caring touch? If you do, it might be an indication that love has crystalized into icy antagonism.

If you find love lacking, touch is an effective and rapid way to reestablish the currents of love. You can transform the desert in your heart into a garden by taking every opportunity to touch.

Hug your children often. Tell them you love them. Touch your close friends. Tell them you care about them. Hold your wife's or husband's hand. Look your lover in the eyes and say it, "*I love you*".

Love is a mighty force. Any attempt to dam it up, hold it back or be stingy with it will produce problems. Conflicts arise, life is filled with adversaries. The dog eat dog, survival of the fittest mentality justifies the misuse and abuse of others.

In order to maintain a solid connection to the spiritual frequencies, love must flow, must radiate into the world. Touching activates love between you and others. When you reduce love or try to hold it back, life begins to fall apart, problems arise one after another. Life becomes a veil of tears.

Experience those joyous moments; touch, hug, hold hands. Experience love's spontaneous exhileration.

Negative,compulsive action
Reduces you to a fraction;
Automatic desire
Fans elemental fire.

Become aware of the urge
Of its sudden surge;
Mechanical mood,
Emotion's food.

Observe anger's flash,
Fiery words rash;
Habitual hate
Seals your fate.

Light Wave 59

Inverted Love

Everyone wants to be loved. Unfortunately, not everyone can give and receive love. In fact, for some, looking for love is a curse. Because of harsh experiences and highly charged memories of those experiences love has inverted.

Inverted love results when love does not flow naturally, warmly and affectionately. Inverted love pooh poohs love. Inverted love laughs sarcastically at love. Inverted love sometimes even believes love does not exist.

People who are gripped by the force of inverted love become harsh, selfish, sensation seekers and insensitive hedonists.

Some years ago I became acquainted with a young woman who suffered from inverted love. A series of negative sexual encounters as a child and teenager had warped her attitude and feelings. Love was pain and suffering to her.

As a result, my friend literally hated love. When she attracted a young man who cared about her, she did everything in her power to turn him off. She was conditioned to repulse love. It was no accident that she had several abortions.

Possessive love is another manifestation of inverted love. On the surface it's hard to detect possessive love since at first glance it looks like genuine unconditional love.

Possessive love is like fools gold. It glitters and shines just like gold but when you try to mold or make it into something beautiful it falls apart.

Possessive love poses and pretends. It imitates true love. Possessive love trys to fool others into believing it loves unconditionally.

In reality, possessive love takes; possessive love is selfish; possessive love looks out for number one. Possessive love manipulates and uses others.

There are many forms of inverted love. Revenge, anger, hatred, resentment, etc. The list goes on and on. The question is how do you Tune into the Spiritual Frequency of love? How do you feel, express and radiate universal, impersonal, unconditional love?

Step 1: Become keenly and acutely aware when you feel-express inverted love energies. When you are jealous, notice you are jealous. Say it like it is, "I am now jealous".

Step 2: Avoid self-condemnation when you feel possessive. It is neither good nor bad, right or wrong. It just is. Notice it. Where do you feel it in your body? What do you feel like doing when you feel possessive?

Step 3: Put your attention on love. Love the plants, the flowers, the trees, the water, the lakes, etc. Show and tell your close friends and family members you love them.

If you were going to die in the next six months wouldn't you want to love more? What are you waiting for? Love now! Forgive and love your enemies. Let go of personal grudges. Why wait? Love now. Love will circle back. It will flow and you will glow.

When you make love a part of your everyday life you will feel whole. You won't feel as scattered, fragile and lost. Love will give meaning to the most mundane task. Love and live. Living without loving is a living death.

Flow of force to the field,
The psyche's ways must yield
To conscious structured-light
And noetic-will might.

Channel the force on high,
Psychic images die;
Evolution's course
Returning to the source.

Lift forces thru the head.
Impulsive actions dead;
Noetic being,
Universal seeing.

Light Wave 60

Why Sci-Art?

Integrating the head, heart and hand in love is a sci-art. To experience any one or two without the third de-stablizes love. All three must be present and interrelated in measured proportion for love to find it's most joyous expression.

Love is a science because it requires intelligence, awareness and timing. Intelligence implies a mind that can weigh the facts. Awareness can register and record the other person's changing psychological condition as well as kr.owing one's own psychological state. Timing means knowing when and when not to give.

Love is an art because it requires sensitivity, intuition and spontaneity. Sensitivity is the subtle interchange of feeling. Intuition guides love with unpredictable insights. Spontaneity keeps love alive in the moment.

Love:

Science
- Intelligence
- Awareness
- Timing

Art
- Intuition
- Sensitivity
- Spontaneity

Have you ever experienced a conflict between the head and heart (sci-art) in love? On the one hand the intellect thinks and thinks and thinks, trying to figure out a relationship's pros and cons. On the other hand, the heart starts pumping with torrents of feeling.

When you're caught up in the head you become confused and frustrated. You begin to doubt whether the relationship will lead anywhere. You pile up reasons for and against the relationship. Sometimes you can think yourself right out of a loving relationship. Other times you can think your way into an unloving relationship.

When your heart blazes with attraction and passion, intelligence, awareness and timing are reduced to ashes. The love tide is high. Why consider love's low tide? All that counts is the thrill, the excitement and the exhilaration.

The fiery heart can burn itself out. Then what? The law of the pendulum prevails. Love is at low tide. The head takes over. The loved one is not so great afterall.

The head-heart conflict unbalances love. Love runs hot and cold. Why not mix hot and cold so love runs warm?

When you find yourself thinking too much, balance with feeling. Be more intuitive, sensitive and spontaneous. When you notice yourself feeling too much, use your head. Be more intelligent, aware and timely.

Balanced love leads to the spiritual frequencies. Unbalanced love detunes you from the spiritual frequencies. Balanced love will regenerate and rejuvenate you. Unbalanced love will degenerate and deplete you.

Love is a powerful force. It's not easy harnessing it's power flexibly. It can be done. The effort is well worth it.

Balanced love is most fulfilling and satisfying. You will find your love expressed in so many more ways. You will love more people and more people will love you.

Summary

1. Love is an energy (lovergy) that can be felt and expressed.
2. Lovergy integrates mind-psyche-body.
3. No matter how upset you are tune into lovergy. Hold your attention on love. Love the sky, the sea, the trees, the earth. Love everything and everyone.
4. There are roadblocks to love including hate, resentment, anger, pride, rigid thoughts, fear.
5. The fantasy of love is never the reality of love.
6. Love is a force. When you are in the present with another, love can be felt almost instantaneously.
7. Once you become aware love is everywhere, you want to give what you can, not just take all you can get.
8. It's better to have loved and been hurt than never loved at all.
9. Love knows when to give more, less or not at all.
10. Relationships release energy. A conscious love takes the energy exchange impersonally. Conscious love does not automatically reduce love to romantic or sexual love.
11. Unless there is spiritual and mental compatibility as well as emotional and physical compatibility, there is little if any chance the relationship will last more than a few months.
12. The interchange of lovergy is most immediate when touching, hugging or holding hands. Invisible currents of love energy flow with a caring touch.
13. Experience joyous moments - touch, hug, hold hands. Experience love's spontaneous exhileration.
14. Inverted love results when love does not flow naturally, warmly and affectionately. Inverted love pooh poohs love. Inverted love laughs sarcastically at love.
15. People who are gripped by the force of inverted love become harsh, selfish, sensation seekers and insensitive hedonists.

16. If you were going to die in the next six months wouldn't you want to love more? What are you waiting for? Love now! Forgive and love your enemies. Let go of personal grudges. Why wait? Love now! Love will circle back. It will flow and you will glow.

17. Love is a science because it requires intelligence, awareness and timing. Love is an art because it requires intuition, sensitivity and spontaneity.

18. The heart-head conflict unbalances love. Love runs hot and cold. Why not mix hot and cold so love runs warm?

19. Balanced love leads to the spiritual frequencies. Unbalanced love detunes you from the spiritual frequencies.

Chapter 13

The Science of Health and Healing

What Is The Medical Myth?

It is the religiously automatic belief that modern medical practices can or will cure every disease, disorder or disagreeable physical problem.

How many people do you know run to the doctor at the slightest physical pain? A person has a headache or a stomach ache. They run to the doctor. The doctor says, "Take two aspirin and rest".

Much too often people project god-like attributes into and onto the doctor. He or she is all-knowing and all-powerful. Many abdicate their knowledge and power, letting the doctor lead the way. They cannot even take care of a headache or stomach ache without consulting a doctor.

For many the medical myth bubble has already burst. They have found out from firsthand experience that the doctor can make a mistake, sometimes even a fatal one. Most everyone today has at least heard of a medical malpractice. Some of the instances sound outlandish and downright horrifying.

Today the medical myth is dying - doctors, the medical profession, are beginning to fall into hard times. People are more cautious; they are asking more questions. Doctors are practicing defensive medicine, ordering more lab tests as protection against malpractice suits. Malpractice insurance premiums have skyrocketed: ten, twenty, thirty, forty, fifty thousand dollars a year and more.

Now, besides projecting god-like qualities on the doctors, we also project devil-like qualities. Many see doctors as greedy, egotistical manipulators who will order more tests and prescribe more drugs just to make more money. Many see doctors as insensitive, uncaring monsters about to make a mistake that will cost someone their life.

Have you ever talked to nurses about doctors? If you ever have the opportunity ask a nurse, "What are the doctors really like?"

Often nurses are cautious about speaking up. They do not want to lose a job; they have family to support.

Most nurses I've met do not have a very high opinion of doctors generally. They use adjectives like dictatorial, demanding, bossy, pompous, rigid, etc. Many nurses will praise a doctor on a professional level but will criticise him/her on a personal level.

Anyway, what does all this talk about the medical myth and the god/devil image of doctors have to do with The Science of Health and Healing? It seems to me that before you or I can take full charge of our health we have to take a look at who we've forfeited our responsibility to: the doctor.

Step one in a valid Science of Health and Healing is to stop projecting god/devil images onto doctors. Doctor 1, is not doctor 2, is not doctor 3. You must judge each doctor individually. If a doctor is required then you must take responsibility for *your* choice.

In my opinion, if you choose a doctor without question simply because the letters M.D. are after his or her name you are partly to blame in the event of malpractice. Stop blaming the doctors. Stop praising the doctors. Stop and look in the mirror.

We must become educated health consumers. You must become your own doctor first. Then, if the need arises, you consult a physician *you* intelligently choose.

Cast off mortal fame
Enbrace immortal flame;
Mind-feelings ignite
With angelic fires bright.

Worldly riches are poor
Without heavenly wealth secure;
Transmute lead to gold
Return to light world's fold.

Invoke archonic power
Purify the lower;
Meditate on the source,
Feel its vibrating force.

Light Wave 61

Health Maintenance

Yesterday I was talking with a chiropractor about his patients. He went through a series of emotions describing their lackluster attitude towards health maintenance. He was amazed, angry, disturbed, confused, disgusted, exasperated, etc.

He discovered in his practice what is true generally about our society: people are more interested in automobile maintenance than in their health maintenance. He falsely believed that because there was so much press about health maintenance his patients would be eager to invest time, money and effort to eliminate future health problems now.

He found out what most health professionals find out: most people wait for the pain. People push themselves, abuse themselves, degenerate themselves and then act as if nothing will happen. Then one day the pain level rises. They run to a health professional expecting instant relief.

What exasperated the chiropractor most were the patients who suffered pain. He relieved them of their pain but they continued to abuse themselves expecting the pain magically never to come back.

He told me of one woman who suffered excruciating back pain. She was rather well to do and could easily afford the visits. She had never gone to a chiropractor before. She had little or no knowledge of health maintenance.

After a series of ten adjustments, which included health maintenance counseling, the woman's pain subsided. Still, the chiropractor explained to the woman that she needed preventive treatment to avoid more pain. She declined further treatments. The pain returned seven months later more excruciating than before.

Health is a dynamic state of physical, emotional, mental and spiritual equilibrium. Physical pain or disease is the final stage of continous unbalanced behavior.

Health maintenance is the attitude-action combination that accepts responsibility for one's health. A health maintenance approach to living acknowledges that health is an ongoing process requiring daily good health habits.

Take a look at the Health Maintenance Dial, figure #5 on page 111. Evaluate yourself in each of the six areas. Grade yourself on a 0-10 scale. Be as honest as you possibly can.

Now add up the six numbers. Your total will give you an approximate indication of your health maintenance level.

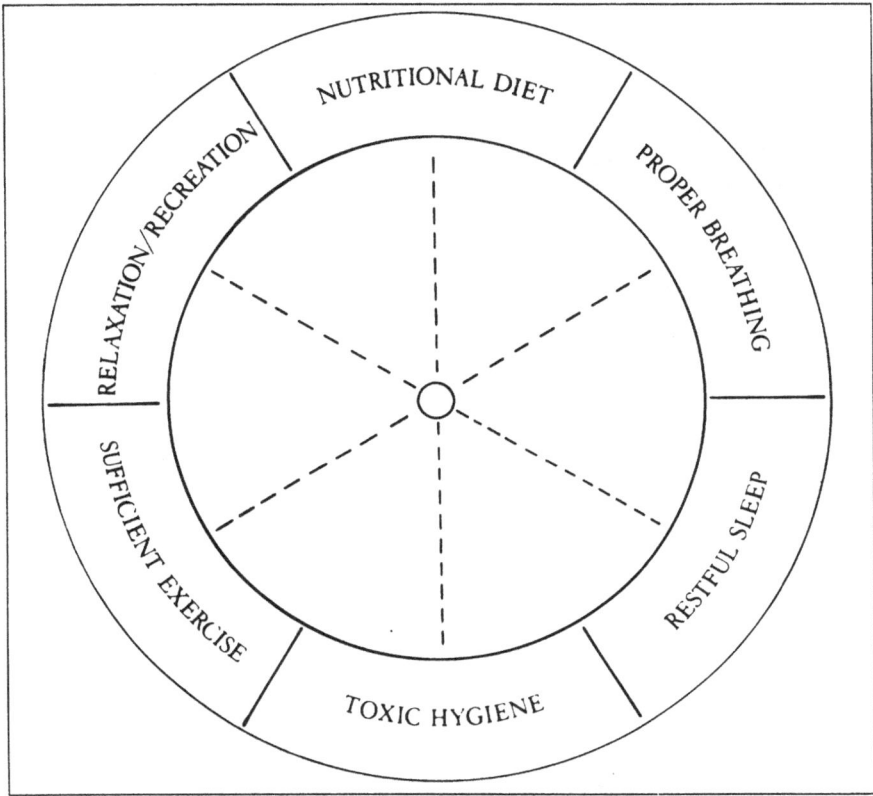

Figure 5: Health Maintenance Dial

Health Maintenance Level

60 .... Perfect
50-59 .... Excellent
35-49 .... Good
20-34 .... Poor
19-Below .... Sickness, Disease, Illness, Dying, Death, etc.

Obviously, if your total is below 35 you're either already sick or have a high potential for illness. You need to take charge now. Why wait till you suffer before taking charge of your health maintenance? Develop and stay on a health maintenance program that is appropriate and comfortable for you.

Start walking if you're not exercising. Improve your nutrition by beginning to use whole grains, reducing your red meat and eliminating processed sugar. Learn some relaxation techniques. Make sure you get plenty of fresh air.

It really doesn't take that much effort. The increased vitality, clarity of mind and feeling of well-being will motivate you to continue raising your health maintenance level.

Being of celestial fire
Transmute my bestial attire;
Burn the mummy form
Till the light body is born.

Dissolve my rigid ways
In liquid light bays;
Cool emotion's heat
In heaven's arctic retreat.

Loosen my earthly ties,
Shine the light on lies;
Remove memory's pain
With love's eternal refrain.

Light Wave 62

The Medical-Wholistic Marriage

For several years I have been receiving news releases from the American Medical Association (AMA). Believe it or not I see signs that the medical profession is moving toward a more wholistic approach.

There are reports on nutrition, exercise and the excessive use of surgery. There is more acceptance of the mental and emotional causes behind disease. Still, the drug therapy emphasis remains.

I see other signs of a medical-wholistic marriage. Many medical doctors are giving up the premise that the body is the source of disease. They are accepting a wholistic premise acknowledging the different human levels: spiritual, mental, emotional, creative, relationships and physical.

The medical profession, somewhere along the way, became fixed on the body. They looked, examined and diagnosed the person as if they were a body only. The medical profession as-a-whole lost its sensitivity to the individual, the whole person.

If the person is just a body with millions of chemical reactions going on then it makes sense to prescribe chemicals to change the reactions. A lot of doctors started making a lot of money prescribing drugs. You can see a steady stream of patients when you send them to the drugstore for their fix.

I did some work for a local doctor, originally from Australia, who integrates medical and wholistic practices. He created the Wellness Game which is marketed across the country. The game is an educational tool emphasizing an integrative, balanced approach to health.

One of my students has always dreamed of becoming a doctor. She wants to bring a wholistic view to her medical training. Right now she is searching for a medical school that integrates body-soul-spirit. She is searching for a medical school that covers alternative health programs like acupressure, relaxation, color, etc.

She hasn't found such a school *yet*. You can be sure she isn't the only one looking for this new age medical school. As the demand gets stronger, the medical schools will change. They will offer alternative therapies and they will emphasize health maintenance.

New age doctors and health professionals will be health maintenance engineers instead of disease mechanics. They will see human beings not as bodies, but as dynamic energy beings. As health maintenance engineers they will be able to spot unbalanced energies and behaviors which may lead to physiological dis-ease months or years down the road.

This will happen because it's too expensive to be sick; it's too expensive to have surgery; it's too expensive to stay in the hospital. The upper middle class and rich are the only ones who can afford health insurance.

Health maintenance education from an early age is the best and least expensive form of health insurance. Let's pray that in the future there will be people who never spend even one day in the hospital.

The fool's fashion,
Profit's passion;
Lost in a godless craze.
Killing over a noise-phrase.

Turn mortal attention
Toward the ascension;
Let go unbalanced ways,
Bask in cosmic rays.

Shower in the blessed fire,
Burn away the liar;
Raise the flaming cross,
Transmute the earthly dross.

Light Wave 63

Light-Energy-Health

Last night I was fortunate to hear a Zen Buddhist priest give a talk at the local YWCA. He said something of great significance which is at the core of this chapter on health and healing. He said, "With a diseased body the mind cannot function and, in turn, meditation becomes very difficult."

Tuning to the Spiritual Frequencies absolutely requires a relatively healthy body. An unhealthy body disturbs the mental field blocking the vibrations of spiritual peace, poise and perception.

There are thousands of books on nutrition, exercise, positive thought and the like which give practical ways to improve your health. I don't need to repeat any of that here. Instead, I'm going to focus on the source of health, the light-energy frequencies.

From birth you are connected to the spiritual dimensions by a ray of light. It enters the so-called physical body through the top of the head, the Door of Bramha to the Hindus.

When you have the opportunity, place your hand above the head of a new-born baby. If you have any degree of sensitivity you'll feel a very definite current or vibration. In a healthy baby this spiritual ray flows continuously into the baby's auric-field and body.

Now, what happens to the current of light once it enters the aura-body? The great scientist Isaac Newton performed an experiment which illustrates what happens to the spiritual ray. He directed a beam of white light to pass through a prism. The result was a separation of light into the spectrum of seven colors.

When the spiritual ray passes into the human being it divides into seven energies. These energy vibrations activate, sustain, energize and maintain your life force. When the spiritual ray and life energies flow unimpeded you are healthy. On the other hand, if there are blocks and resistances to the natural flow of light and energy then an unhealthy condition begins.

This is the foundation of the Science of Health and Healing. New age health maintenance engineers will be more interested in the spiritual light ray and the seven energy currents than the physical symptoms. The symptoms are the result. The energy block is the secondary cause and some misuse or misdirection of energy is the primary cause.

In order to maintain a conscious connection to the Spiritual Frequencies descending and ascending through the top of your head, you must reject altogether a purely physical approach to health. Instead, you must embrace, see, accept and understand an energy view toward health.

An energy view of health sees a headache from a totally different perspective. The spiritual frequency entering the body from a higher dimension has met resistance in the head-energy area. There is a block in the natural energy flow.

What is the cause of this energy blockage called a headache? The general cause is an unconscious identification leading to a misuse or unbalanced use of energy. The specific identification could run the gambit from excessive use of mental energy, negative thinking or a sympathetic vibrational rapport from someone else.

In the next two sections I'm going to give some ways to unblock energy and, as a result, restore its natural healthy flow.

A ray of truth-light
Illumines mind night,
Exposes shadow thought,
In mental glue caught.

Intense regenerate flames
Burns away earthly claims;
Ascended masters guide,
Mortal knots untied.

Spirit's electronic volts,
A matrix of cosmic bolts;
Touch the god-flow
Till mind-body glow.

Light Wave 64

Raising Your Vibration

The master key to maintaining your health is keeping your energy level high. When you make a habit of running yourself down and do nothing to raise your vibrations, you will eventually suffer the consequences.

After repeatedly abusing yourself with too much work, poor nutrition and addictive excesses, the body cells become overloaded with toxins. You suddenly feel drained. Often the ego falsely believes it can do whatever it wants and get away with it.

You stop thinking of yourself as a personality in a physical body. Forget that! Begin focusing on energy. See yourself as an energy being. In fact, it is structurally and functionally more accurate to say you're an energy being than a human being.

As you orient your consciousness to the energy world, it will become necessary to raise your vibrations when your energy is low. There are literally thousands of ways of raising your vibrations. I'm going to present just a few simple, easy to practice methods.

Rhythmic breathing is very effective at raising your energy level. (See Chapter 9: The Science of Breathing). It's so simple people do not really give it much value at first. Test it out. It works like a charm. And besides, it's free.

Sit comfortably wherever you happen to be. I used to practice rhythmic breathing on the subway on my way home from work. Begin observing the natural inhalation and exhalation of breath. Take the air in slowly through the nose, a full breath. Then exhale slowly through the nose. Keep this conscious rhythmic breathing process up for 5-10-15 minutes. By the way rhythmic breathing has been known to relieve a headache from time to time.

Relaxation, it's so easy. (See Chapter 10: The Science of Relaxation). You just have to take time to do it. You can relax anywhere, sitting in the office, standing in line, walking down the street, literally anywhere.

To relax bring your attention to the tension spots. The back of the neck, the jaw, the shoulders, the hips, etc. Feel the tension; release the tension. Slowly rotate the head to the right then to the left.

Creative expression also raises your vibrations. (See Chapter 14: The Science of Creativity). Draw, paint, dance, sing, make music, etc. Please, forget about being a creative genius. Just have fun.

Do you recall how you feel after being creative? I took a class at the local art museum, Drawing on the Right Side of the Brain. After each class I felt lighter, more relaxed, full of energy and more mellow.

Remember, you are an energy being in a dynamic energy world. Often you rush, push, think, feel, emote too much; you lose your vitality. Stop - become conscious of your energy level. Take a break. Breath rhythmically, relax, hum a song -- raise your vibrations.

Across the sea of light,
Of transparent golden-white;
On a ship with solar sails
Passed giant cosmic whales.

Hands of unrelenting will
Holds the golden wheel still;
Forever manning the helm,
Toward the light being realm.

Reaching the edge of divine night
Cosmic presence wields its might,
Dissolves individual form,
Cosmic consciousness born.

Light Wave 65

Heal Yourself

Once you regularly Tune to the Spiritual Frequencies you must assume responsibility for your own health and healing. To relinquish your health and healing responsibility to someone else, especially a medical doctor, could be dangerous to your health.

Why? As you participate, experience, integrate and live in the spiritual frequencies, subtle and fundamental changes occur on the cellular level. Your cells, your blood, your organs, your so-called physical body becomes more sensitive and tuned to the higher vibrations.

Now, because of past misuses of energy in thought, in speech, in feeling and in action, there are unbalanced vibrations in your body. The body cells retain the memory of the unbalanced energy expressions. As you raise your vibrations negative energies are released. Sometimes the body casts off the negative vibrations by a cold, a fever, a stomach disorder, a burning in the back of the neck, etc.

Running to the doctor will be a waste of time, money and energy. They'll find nothing wrong with you in the conventional way. They will not, as a rule, understand the bio-chemical/spiritual process you are going through.

Naturally, you must clearly discriminate a natural cleansing process from an actual bio-physical disorder. If you are attuned you'll know the difference.

Regardless of the ailment's source, you must be your own doctor, heal yourself. That means knowing something about alternative healing methods. Go to your local new age bookstore and look for books on health and healing. You'll find hundreds covering a wide range of alternative treatments.

Reflexology, Bach flowers, cell salts, gems, herbs, color, nutrition, vitamins, magnets, rhythmic breathing. You could make a list a page long. The question is, how do you know which therapy or therapies to use to heal yourself?

The process of knowing which therapy to use begins with familiarizing yourself with a variety of alternative methods. I would suggest building up a small library specializing in health and healing. Try some of the methods on yourself so you can get a feel for their uses. Finally, you must be receptive, intuitive and aware. The correct method or methods will spontaneously arise in your consciousness.

Whatever self-healing techniques you use, please remember to continue Tuning to the Spiritual Frequencies. You can get so wrapped up playing doctor to yourself you lose the connection to the master healing force.

The current of light, love, wisdom descending from the spiritual dimensions is the master healing force. Hold your attention on it. Feel the regenerational currents vibrate throughout your body. Feel it's rejuvenating process heal and restore balance to the body.

Sometimes you must go through a cleansing process. There may not be a whole lot you can do about it. Be patient. Hold your attention on the light. Know that you're going through the healing process.

During these times, which may be very uncomfortable, watch your thoughts and emotions. You may start to worry that something terrible is wrong with you. You may get depressed and wonder if the cleansing powers will ever pass. Get your thoughts and feelings back on track.

Remember, you are no longer identified with the body as all you are. You are a spiritual being learning to function in an energy world.

Summary

1. The medical myth is the automatic belief that medical practices can or will cure every disease, disorder or disagreeable physical problem.
2. If you choose a doctor without question simply because the letters M.D. are after his or her name, you are to blame in the event of malpractice.
3. We must become educated health consumers. You must become your own doctor first. Then, if the need arises, contact a physician you intelligently choose.
4. People push themselves, abuse themselves, degenerate themselves and then act as if nothing will happen. Then one day the pain level rises. They run to a health professional expecting instant relief.
5. Health is a dynamic state of physical, emotional, mental and spiritual equilibrium. Physical pain or disease is the final stage of continuous unbalanced behavior.
6. A health maintenance approach to living acknowledges that health is an ongoing process requiring daily good health habits.
7. Many medical doctors are giving up the premise that the body is the source of disease. They are accepting a wholistic premise acknowledging the different human levels: spiritual, mental, emotional, creative, relationship and physical.
8. New age doctors and health professionals will be health maintenance engineers instead of disease mechanics.
9. Health maintenance education from an early age is the best and least expensive form of health insurance.
10. Tuning to the Spiritual Frequencies requires a relatively healthy body. An unhealthy body disturbs the mental field blocking the vibrations of spirtual peace, poise and perception.
11. When the spiritual light ray and life energies flow unimpeded you are healthy. On the other hand, if there are blocks and resistances to the natural flow of light and energies then an unhealthy condition begins.

12. The physical symptons are the result. The energy block is the secondary cause and some misuse or misdirection of energy is the primary cause.
13. The master key to maintaining your health is keeping your energy level high.
14. As you orient your consciousness to the energy world it will become necessary to raise your vibrations when your energy is low.
15. Rhythmic breathing, relaxation and creative expression are simple, easily practiced ways of raising your vibrations.
16. As you anticipate, experience, integrate and live in the Spiritual Frequencies subtle and fundamental changes occur on the cellular level.
17. You must be your own doctor; listen to your body. Learn something about alternative healing methods.
18. The current of light, love, wisdom descending from the spiritual dimensions is the master healing force.
19. Remember, you are no longer identified with the body as all you are. You are a spiritual being learning to function in an energy world.

Chapter 14

The Science of Creativity

The Creative Process: Universally

From dimension to dimension and throughout the universe the creative process has remarkable similarities. Whether you're looking at the creation of atomic elements in the stars or thought-forms in the mind, the creative process follows a regular pattern.

The different states H_2O takes under different conditions illustrates the creative process universally. When the water molecules rush about at boiling or above, water turns into steam or water vapor. Water is then in a gaseous state; its most etheric condition. The creative process is an emergence of substance from etheric to concrete and then a return to an etheric state.

When the water molecules in the gaseous state slow down their activity below the boiling point, H_2O returns to its liquid form. Relative to our senses something has emerged out of nothing. Water has condensed from an invisible gaseous state to a visible liquid.

As the liquid H_2O condenses further and the molecules slow down even more, water becomes ice. The H_2O molecules have crystalized into a solid substance. The creative process has reached its destination and now must make the return trip to complete the cycle.

In the dead of winter on Lake Minnetonka just outside of Minneapolis, the lake is frozen solid. The snow crunches underfoot at 20 below. The wind pierces through your down jacket like invisible icicles. The ice is so thick on the lake that cars travel across it without a problem.

A few months pass. Spring comes. The temperature rises. The ice melts. No more driving on Lake Minnetonka. The ice covering the lake changes back to liquid water.

The cool spring air feels warm blowing across the face after the sting of winter. Life emerges, becoming more active. The trees and flowers bud. The grass turns green. Before long its summer on Lake Minnetonka. Hot and muggy, it becomes almost impossible to sleep at night. The humidity is so high that H_2O saturates the air with gaseous water vapor.

Using the seasonal changes of water from winter, to spring to summer as a dramatization of the creative process, H_2O closes the circle of creation. Gas, liquid, solid - steam, water, ice; solid, liquid, gas - ice, water, steam - Lake Minnetonka winter, spring, summer - you can almost feel the creative process.

The stars are born out of whirling interstellar gases that heat up and light up. They radiate starlight for a billion years, then burn out. The gases dispurse through the endless heavens eventually becoming part of the substance forming a new star across the galaxy.

Birth, life, death and rebirth is the never-ending cycle of creation. From breath to breath, from heartbeat to heartbeat, we are a living creative process interconnected with every other creative process following archetypal geometric patterns.

The unconscious sleep,
The suffering weep;
Screen of illusion,
Mindless confusion.

An event quickens,
The psyche awakens;
Glimpses of light,
Moments of flight.

The quick and the dead,
Put on the actor's head;
Play the role
While becoming whole.

Light Wave 66

The Creative Process: Individually

Mary is an artist. She draws, paints and handicrafts. The creative process is a center in her life.

Let's pretend we can zoom into Mary's mind, psyche and body. With our clairvoyant vision and acute sensitivity to vibrations, we follow Mary's immediate experience through a creative process.

1. First we feel a deep inexplicable urge within. Some compelling force to do something creative courses through Mary's veins. She doesn't know what she wants to create but she knows she wants to create.

2. Suddenly a flash, then another and another. The mind glows; the brain currents flicker and flame. An idea, a thought - Mary knows she wants to draw. She doesn't know yet what she wants to draw but she knows for sure she wants to draw.

3. A few seconds pass, a minute, two minutes. The thought begins to take shape. It becomes clearer and clearer and clearer. A flower! That's it. Mary wants to draw a flower. The flower in her mind doesn't look like any particular flower. It's a kind of universal flower - every flower. Wow! Things are really getting active in here now. Electrical currents are flowing at the speed of light.

4. Nerves are flickering on and off like fireflys. Muscles are twittering, stretching and contracting. Mary is taking constructive action. She picks up her drawing pad and pencils. She sits down at her favorite table and opens her sketch book. She stares into the blank page. It's 9 x 12 inches. She knows the drawing will be within those limits.

5. As Mary's mind turns the pages of her memory searching for a flower to draw she gets herself into a creative mood.

6. She feels a peace, a calm and a harmony. She becomes receptive to the moment. She takes a deep breath. Her muscles relax poised for creative activity.

7. Suddenly, a brilliant white daisy forms in her mind. The shape, the color, the design, the texture - this daisy is a living hologram of the daisy in the vase on the table.

8. Streams of light pass through the optic nerve to the brain. The image of the daisy has left the mental field. The radiant streams of light enter the mind and begin forming little bits and pieces of the daisy.

9. Mary is visually abstracting every detail. Now there's an intense flurry of activity for about 30 minutes. The eyes scan, jump, part, stare and blink. The hand grasps the pencil, flows across the paper, stops, moves slightly and glides on.

10. Presto! There's a beautiful pencil drawing of the daisy. It looks similar to the daisy in the vase but different. We feel mixed emotions in Mary, some satisfaction, some dissatisfaction.

To review, here are the 10 creative steps Mary went through from beginning to end.
1. A creative urge.
2. A creative idea.
3. A clear creative idea.
4. Constructive creative action.
5. Setting creative limits.
6. Getting into a creative mood.
7. A specific creative idea.

8. A detailed creative plan.
9. Creative activity.
10. Creation.

Whether drawing, painting, dancing, singing, playing an instrument - no matter the creative activity, the creative process follows a similar pattern. Begin plugging into this creative process and tapping the creative energies that flow from the creative source in the spiritual dimensions. Creative energies are Spiritual Frequencies.

> *Psychic nature churning,*
> *Conscious learning;*
> *Raise the psychic urge,*
> *With the noetic merge.*
>
> *Across a vast abyss,*
> *Aglow with light's bliss;*
> *Alone, no going back*
> *To the world of lack.*
>
> *Light transmutation,*
> *Intense regeneration;*
> *Every sinew and cell*
> *Cleansed of the psyche's hell.*
>
> *Light Wave 67*

The Right Side Of The Brain

There's been a lot said and written in recent years about left and right brain functions. The left side of the brain has to do with linear, logical thinking and activity. The right side of the brain has to do with non-linear, creative thinking and activity.

I'm not going to rewrite what's already been written about right brain/left brain functions. The library and bookstores have plenty to read. Instead, I'm going to tell you about my experience taking a class at the Sierra Nevada Museum of Art, "Drawing on the Right Side of the Brain".

Let me describe some of the things we did to stimulate right brain activity which resulted in the flow of creative energy.

Our teacher, Kathy, handed us an object under the table while our eyes were closed. Once we had the object in hand, we could open our eyes. While touching the object, we had to draw it.

The rational left brain wanted desperately to see the object. You had the thought, "How can I draw something I can't see?" As a result, though, the right brain was forced into activity.

At another class Kathy asked us to draw something upside down. She gave us all the same picture and placed it upside down on the table in front of us. We proceeded to draw. After completing the drawing we turned it rightside up. A lot of the drawings looked as good as if they were drawn the "normal" way.

Still another exercise required us to draw objects without looking at the paper. We would place the pencil point on the paper, look at the object to be drawn and then draw without looking at the paper. Some of the drawings were quite interesting. You could even recognize what the object was.

Anyway, I know you're getting the point. The class approached drawing from a totally unexpected, illogical, unconventional direction. The unexpected, illogical, unconventional are all right brain functions.

The classes were in the evening after a long work day. Usually I felt tired and tense when I came to class. By the time the class was over I felt energized and relaxed. In fact, I felt time had slipped into timelessness.

As I left each week I felt "spaced out". I tended to linger awhile talking to the other people in the class. I almost felt like I was floating or like I was walking on air.

When we left the museum I heard comments like, "Isn't that tree beautiful", "Look at that cloud formation", "The sunset is spectacular".

It seems the senses become more acute after tapping creative energies. Form, color, shape, texture and relations are more vivid to the eye.

I enjoyed Kathy's class so much I took the next one, Drawing on the Right Side of the Brain, Color. Each week we would take another color and explore. The class focused more on sensing, feeling, perceiving color than on technique, although we learned some technique as well.

After taking these classes I realized how the left brain, logical, linear thinking blocks the flow of creative energies. The left brain has all kinds of reasons why you cannot draw or paint. I can't do it; it doesn't look right, I don't know what to draw, I'm not an artist, etc.

Rediscovering the spontaneous, playful realm of creating that we had continuous access to as a child opens channels to the spiritual frequencies.

We become the creative process. We are the creative process. Creative energies course through us again revitalizing and making us whole.

Conscious function is the way
Transforms night to day;
Feel noetic light,
Burns intensely bright.

Structure consciously the day,
Strait and narrow the way;
Tune to Christ force,
On the cosmic course.

Consciously order the pathway,
Spiral toward the light of day;
Guided by the master power,
Till the jewel crowned hour.

Light Wave 68

Inspiration - Perspiration

Inspiration is the initial creative thrust. It's the force that lights up your mind, heart and soul. Inspiration makes you feel good. Your spirit soars. You are Tuning to a Spiritual Frequency.

It's difficult to say what's going to inspire you - a dream, a sunset, a song, a lover, a sunrise, a thundershower, a painting - the list goes on forever. Inspiration is spontaneous, exhilerating and often motivates you to create.

The creative flash may ignite a thought to create most anything from a poem to a new invention. How often do you follow through with the creative flash? When you're filled with the inspirational charge do you channel that energy into creative work?

I am currently writing this book. Of course, now that you're reading it, it's sometime in the past that I wrote it. Still, the energy and effort it took to write this book spanned hundreds of hours.

As I write this book I have a list of book ideas written in a notebook. Each was an inspiration. Right now there are eight book ideas forming, simmering and filtering in the back of my mind.

I can recall the tremendous lift I got when I received the inspiration to write each book on the list. I was swept up in a dynamic vortex of thought, feeling and excitement. Sometimes the inspirational process lasted a few minutes and sometimes it came on and off over a few weeks.

I would estimate the total time of inspiration for the eight future books was less than ten hours. The effort, energy and perspiration to produce those eight books will require hundreds, even thousands of hours. Hours and hours of research, contemplation, writing, re-writing, editing, manuscript preparation, book production will go into each project.

Fortunately, over the years I've written many of the inspirational ideas down. Many I have not written down and are lost or possibly taken up by someone else. I would say for every inspiration I have written down in seed-thought form there are five to ten inspirations I have not written down.

The point is obvious. Creative inspiration is one percent of the creative process; creative perspiration is the other 99 percent of the creative process. Thomas Edison was inspired to create the electric lightbulb. He probably wasn't the first to be inspired with such a vision. But he was the first to meticulously test some 10,000 substances as filaments in an electric lightbulb until he hit on the substance that lit up the world.

I know people who are bubbling with creative thought. They love to tell you all about their latest inspiration - an invention, a book, a song, etc. A year or two later they're still talking about some new idea. Often, they cannot even remember the ones from the past. It is not unusual for these people to be disappointed to find someone else was inspired with a similar idea and followed through on it.

Watch your speech. If you want to create take care not to dissipate the creative energies in excited speech. Sure it feels good temporarily but when it comes time to apply effort to the creative process all the wind could be out of your sails.

I've opened my big mouth on many occasions only to be discouraged and even depressed later because I've blown the initial charge of creative energy. If possible, you're better off jotting down a few notes. Once you've created, talk about it all you want.

Steer a natural course,
Spiraling toward the source;
Steady the psychic storm
Shape the archetypal form.

Concentrate on the field,
Keep your lips sealed;
Experience vital power,
Feel elementals cower.

Meditate on the now,
Stop asking how;
Grow turn by turn,
Live what you learn.

Light Wave 69

The Superconscious Hotline

Whatever you create, whether it's a scrumptious meal, a beautiful sweater or a soaring sculpture, you feel better. Something shifts within you. The energies change. Creativity is a hotline to the superconscious spiritual frequencies.

Can you believe it? It's so simple. All you have to do is create and you tune into spiritual vibrations. And, guess what, your creation does not have to be perfect, exceptional or the best. If you enjoyed tapping the creative energies then you'll feel better.

If you're a creative person already you know what I'm talking about. Musicians, artists, dancers, writers, craftspeople know how good they feel during creative activity and after. A kind of whole, balanced, inner contented feeling comes over you. That's how the superconscious vibrations feel to the mind-body, conscious-subconscious and intellect-instincts.

For those of you who do not experience the flow of creative energies regularly decide now to tap your creative potential. Tuning to the Spiritual Frequencies can be accomplished so easily through creativity. And it's fun too!

Naturally it's easier said than done. Many have subconscious blocks to creativity. I've heard people say: "I can't draw", "I'm not creative", "I tried but I was terrible", etc. Everybody is creative. Everybody has some special talent or talents.

Have you ever noticed the spontaneous outpouring of creative energy from your children? If you have kids, you know what I'm talking about. They haven't been made to feel they cannot create.

When my boy, Dane, was two, he loved to dance, sing, play the piano and the harmonica. We did not discourage his spontaneous feelings. Naturally, his dance movements were not the result of training. Obviously, he did not play recognizable songs on the piano. Who cared. He was in a joyful place. He was tapping creative energies. It felt good.

He didn't feel inferior, ashamed, shy, uptight or apprehensive about creating. In fact, he didn't even have a concept of creativity. He just created.

If there is little or no creativity in your life then you probably have a subconscious block. A teacher, a parent, a friend, a brother, a sister or someone has made you feel like you cannot sing, dance, draw, etc., etc. You became self-conscious; you blocked the natural flow of creative energies.

You do not have to be Picasso, Barbra Streisand, Dustin Hoffman -- the great master artist. Forget that. All you have to do is play, have a good time, enjoy yourself.

Judging creativity as you're creating, blocks the natural flow of creative energies. Create now; judge or evaluate later, if you must.

Most everyone has secretly wanted to do something creative. Maybe it was build something out of wood, craft jewelry or play the guitar. Whatever the secret yearning - try it. See what happens.

There are classes on just about anything you can think of right in your community. Call the high school, community college, YMCA, YWCA -- start networking, you'll find a class just for you.

Public televison offers a number of classes which can assist you in tapping creative energies: painting, dancing, piano, cooking, do-it-yourself around the house, etc.

Stop procrastinating; at your earliest convenience give it a try. An hour a week isn't too much to ask of yourself.

Notice how good you feel. Forget results. Forget about how "good" or how "bad". That's not important. The creative currents are a hotline to the superconscious spiritual frequencies.

> *Noetic consciousness awake,*
> *Maya psyche is fake;*
> *False-word-image-thing*
> *Pain-suffering bring.*
>
> *There is another path*
> *Beyond the psychic wrath;*
> *It demands heroic will*
> *And god-mind still.*
>
> *It follows cosmic laws*
> *Not man-made flaws;*
> *Personal desire overcome,*
> *Thy will be done.*
>
> *Light Wave 70*

Creators - Maintainers - Destroyers

There are three types of people in the world: *Creators, Maintainers* and *Destroyers.*

The creative person, as we have been describing in the last few pages taps creative energies manifesting inventions, songs, paintings, systems, discoveries, novels, etc.

The maintainer is the responsible everyday person who works hard, pays their bills, raises children, lives in houses, etc.

The destroyer is the irresponsible person, the criminal, the thief, the murderer, the terrorist. The destroyer tears down what the creators create and what the maintainers maintain.

Now each type has three types as follows:

Creator
- Creator/Creator
- Creator/Maintainer
- Creator/Destroyer

Maintainer
- Maintainer/Creator
- Maintainer/Maintainer
- Maintainer/Destroyer

Destroyer
- Destroyer/Creator
- Destroyer/Maintainer
- Destroyer/Destroyer

I'm not going to go into a complete explanation of the nine types of people at this time. Instead, I'll focus on creative people generally.

This story will make my point. After graduating from high school, Sam did not know what he wanted to do for a living. In high school he excelled in theatre. He was outstanding in every play he was in. In his heart, he wanted to continue in theatre in some way.

He dreamed of Hollywood. He dreamed of Broadway. He dreamed of getting into the local theatre company.

His mom and dad, who were honest, hard-working bill-payers, did not encourage his theatrical "hobby". Dad owned and operated a successful jewelry store and expected Sam to come into the business after college. Both mom and dad suggested studying economics, business, marketing, so Sam could bring some new financial know-how to the family business.

Sam gave it the old college try. His first year of college was total misery. He knew he should not be there but he didn't want to displease his parents. In his second year, Sam dropped out. He felt lost, lonely and totally discouraged. Mom and dad really showed their disappointment.

He worked in the jewelry store for a while. Then he heard about a college in a nearby state which had a theatre department. He saved his money, applied, was accepted and went to the new college paying his own way. Mom and dad did not support him in his decision.

After graduation from college, he joined a theatre company. He earned a living in theatre as an actor and director. He wasn't a Broadway or Hollywood star, but he was following his heart. He was fulfilling his creative destiny. Mom and dad could never really understand Sam's "rash" behavior.

Creators, maintainers and destroyers tend not to mix that well. Each type sees the world differently and has great difficulty understanding the other types.

If a creative person like Sam trys to become a maintainer like his mom and dad he dooms himself to suffering. He becomes like the square that does not fit into the round hole.

Maintainers admire and respect a financially successful creative person but usually consider a struggling creative person as a misguided soul. Often a maintainer will think a struggling creative person will some day wake up, realize his or her mistake and get back into the "real" world.

It is critical that a creative person spend time with other creative people in order to keep the creative energies flowing consistently.

Summary

1. Whether you're looking at the creation of atomic elements in the stars or thought-forms in the mind, the creative process follows a regular pattern.

2. The creative process is an emergence of substance from super-subtle etheric energies to concrete matter and then a return to an etheric state.

3. Birth, life, death and rebirth is the never-ending cycle of creation. From breath to breath, from heartbeat to heartbeat, we are a living creative process.

4. On an individual level the ten creative steps are: a creative urge, a creative idea, a clear creative idea, constructive creative action, setting creative limits, getting into a creative mood, a specific creative idea, a detailed creative plan, creative activity and creation.

5. Whether drawing, painting, dancing, singing, playing an instrument -- no matter the creative activity, the creative process follows a similar pattern.

6. Plug into the creative process. Tap the creative energies. Creative energies are spiritual frequencies.

7. The left side of the brain has to do with linear, logical thinking and activity. The right side of the brain has to do with non-linear, creative thinking and activity.

8. The Drawing on the Right Side of the Brain class approached drawing from a totally unexpected, illogical, unconventional direction.

9. By the time the class was over I felt energized and relaxed. My senses became more acute. Form, color, shape, texture and relations were more vivid.

10. Inspiration is the initial creative thrust; it's the force that lights up your mind, heart and soul. Inspiration is spontaneous, exhilerating and often motivates you to create.

11. Creative inspiration is one percent of the creative process; creative perspiration is the other 99 percent of the creative process.

12. Watch your speech. If you want to create, take care not to dissipate the creative energies in excited speech. Once you've created, talk about it all you want.

13. Creativity is a hotline to the superconscious spiritual frequencies. During creativity and after, a kind of whole, balanced, inner contented feeling comes over you.

14. Many have subconscious blocks to creativity. I've heard people say, "I can't draw", "I'm not creative", "I tried but I was terrible", etc. Everybody is creative. Everybody has some special talent or talents.

15. You do not have to be Picasso, Barbra Streisand, Dustin Hoffman -- forget that. All you have to do is play, have a good time, enjoy yourself.
16. There are three types of people in the world: Creators, Maintainers and Destroyers.
17. Creators, maintainers and destroyers tend not to mix that well. Each type sees the world differently and has great difficulty understanding the other types.
18. When creative people spend too much time around maintainers and destroyers their creative juices tend to stop flowing. They are cut off, to some extent, from the spiritual frequencies.

Chapter 15

The Science of Color

The Color Spectrum

Draw a rainbow. It will assist you in learning more about color. You'll need colored pencils or crayons, paper and a compass.

With the compass make seven concentric half circles. (See figure #6 on page 133).

Now color them in. Make the largest half circle red. Continue as follows: orange, yellow, green, blue, indigo, and violet.

The colors in your rainbow appear in the same order as in a natural rainbow after a rain storm. Why? Let's journey back in time about three hundred years to the laboratory of Sir Isaac Newton, one of the world's greatest scientists.

We see Newton experimenting with light and prisms. He sets up a prism and shines white light through it. Amazingly a color spectrum appears. The white light separates into seven colors in exactly the same order as the colors in both the natural rainbow and in the rainbow you drew.

Light, then, is energy vibrating at different wavelengths. In the visible light spectrum we see these energy wavelengths as color. A wavelength is the distance from crest to crest of a vibration. The wave frequency is the number of waves in a specific time period.

Now, the shorter the wavelength the higher the frequency. The longer the wavelength the lower the frequency. Red has the longest wavelength in the color spectrum, twenty-eight millionth of an inch. Violet, at the other end of the spectrum, has the shortest wavelength, sixteen millionth of an inch. You see long and short are indeed relative terms.

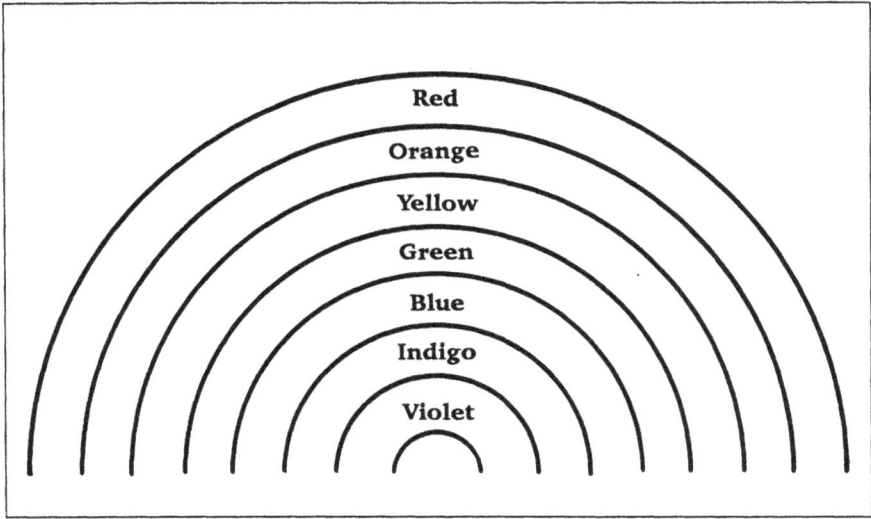

Figure 6: The Rainbow Spectrum

Look at figure #7 on page 134, The Electromagnetic Spectrum. Notice that visible color is but a narrow slit in the spectrum. There is far more that is invisible than there is visible.

If you contemplate this diagram for a few minutes something staggering dawns in your mind. You discover your sense of sight is extremely limited. There is much more that you do not see than what you can see.

Glance at the spectrum once again. Notice x-rays have a relatively high frequency (short wavelengths) and radio waves a relatively low frequency (long wavelengths). We know that too much exposure to x-rays can cause serious physiological difficulties. You cannot see or feel them! At this very moment there are radio waves from several radio stations moving through the room you are in. You cannot hear anything until a radio is turned on!

Webster defines color as the sensation resulting from stimulation of the retina of the eye by light waves of certain lengths. We see a color, for instance blue, because a blue surface absorbs all colors and reflects the blue wavelength to our eye. White is the presence of all colors and therefore reflects all colors to the eyes.

Becoming more color conscious is an excellent way to enter into the energy world. Begin noticing colors. Take a different color each day. Observe as many hues and shades as possible. Note the color of objects and natural things.

What do you feel after focusing on a particular color for a while? Do you feel energized, active, hyper, relaxed, calm, or peaceful? Notice your behavior after concentrating on a specific color.

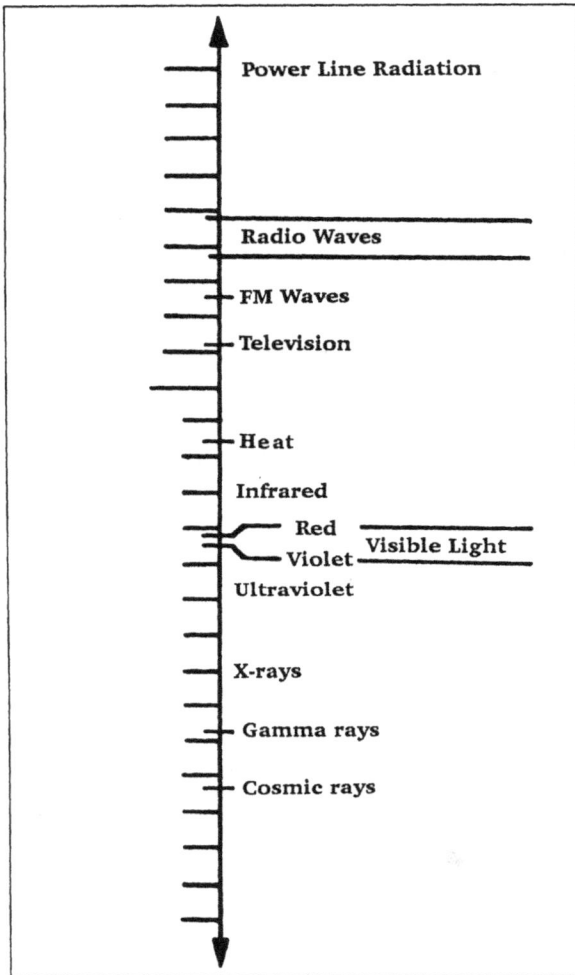

Figure 7: The Electromagnetic Spectrum

I am pointing you toward direct experience and away from mere theory. If color is light and light is energy then you can register and experience color energies.

Do you have a favorite color? Did you ever ask yourself why? Could it be you're not only seeing the color but absorbing the vibrations of that color?

Cosmic perceptions,
Thought-thing reflections;
Higher force flows,
Ignites light halos.

See-feel the three
In the 360 degree;
Positive-negative united,
Continuous creation lighted.

The cosmic pattern repeated
Each thought-action reseeded;
Spiraling vortex grows
Till the source it knows.

Light Wave 71

The Color Chorus

I heard it once said that there are more stars in the heavens than there are grains of sand on the earth. When you talk color, you're talking limitless hues and shades. Within the space of my desk I just observed 16 shades of red. There are many more, I'm sure, I did not observe.

In this section I will describe the main singers in the color chorus. Remember the colors in the rainbow? All I'm going to do here is give some feeling about each color in order to open up vast color ranges.

Red   The stop light turns red. The stop sign is red. You turn red when you sunburn. You cut yourself; you bleed. You're embarrassed; you blush.

How does red feel? Red doesn't put you asleep! It wakes you up. You're more alert. It's hot; it burns.

Have you ever seen red? I mean have you ever gotten fiery, enraged, outraged or angry? Has anyone ever raised your ire?

Orange   Have you had a glass of orange juice lately? Perhaps this morning for breakfast. Have you ever had a glass of orange juice before going to sleep?

Fall is in the air. The nights are cool and crisp. The days are Indian summer. The fields are ripe with pumpkin and squash.

Halloween is spooky, fun, exciting. Trick or Treat? Everyone is wearing a disguise, a costume, a mask. Revelry - do what you like - frolic.

Yellow   It's noon in the desert in August. The sun shines - a radiating ball of yellow nuclear light.

Crack open an egg. Plop - hear it sizzle on the hot grill. Do you like yours sunnyside up?

The light turns yellow. Think! Go or stop. You have a choice; make your decision.

Green Spring time, all the world is bathed in green. Life, growth, peace and love. The leaves, the grasses, the shrubs, even the weeds display their finest green fashion.

As you sit under an old oak on the grass, you relax. You take a break from the hustle and bustle. You forget what time it is. Your mind grazes on nourishing thoughts.

Blue After lying under the old tree for a while your eyes turn skyward. The vast blue ocean of air deepens your peace and serenity. Staring into the cloudless sky the endless blue cools and soothes.

You're feeling blue, a mood, a feeling, an emotion. The depths of an experience stir within. The feeling passes. The pressure is gone. The tension is gone. You forget.

Indigo In the evening the sky darkens, the blue deepens. It's the twilight between day and night. As the sun sets, a palette of colors are displayed. Indigo is made up of orange, green, blue, red and purple.

You gather your thoughts. You collect yourself. Everything makes sense. You see things in their proper perspective. You understand. You know. You forgive.

Violet It's night time. The door to your imagination opens. Enchanted worlds, fantasy lands, magical dreams --violet inspires you to create something from nothing.

Your imagination soars with the phoenix. Visions of art, music and poetry fill your mind! The muses dance in your heart.

The unknown is no longer forbidding, thick with fear. Instead, it is transformed into a wonderland, a realm of infinite possibility.

White A billion stars twinkle in the night, white light. All seven colors sing in unison, a beautiful harmony. Your heart is purified. You are ready for a new day.

> *Crystalline light*
> *Shimmers bright,*
> *Rejuvenates cells,*
> *Burns out hells.*
>
> *Diamond light*
> *Dissolves night,*
> *Transmutes thought,*
> *Universes wrought.*
>
> *Neutron light,*
> *So bright it's night,*
> *Transforms essence*
> *Into God's Presence.*
>
> *Light Wave 72*

Color Breathing

Breathing and color, what a wonderful combination. Both are powerful rejuvenators. Whether you're feeling down, tired, hyper, rushed - whatever the unbalanced state, color breathing is an excellent way to restore your equilibrium.

How in the world does one color breath? Visualization plus rhythmic breathing equals color breathing.

In the beginning, I suggest you choose a quiet spot, a peaceful moment and a comfortable place to sit. Maybe, at first, avoid the couch or easy chair. Sit in a chair where you must sit up straight.

Now relax the shoulders - neck - jaw - wherever you're tense. Close your eyes if you like. I prefer to keep mine open. Choose a color; let's try white.

When you visualize white in your mind's eye see it as vibrant, electric, alive - as white light. Visualize that vibrant white light in you, through you, around you.

Now you're ready to breath color. Become aware, as you maintain your visualization, of the natural rise and fall, in and out of your breathing. Breath through the nose.

On the in-breath visualize the electric white-light-air streaming into your lungs through your nostrils. See your lungs filling with this white color energy then expanding rapidly through the blood stream to every cell of the body. Then, in your own natural breathing rhythm exhale slowly through the nose. Visualize nothing on the out-breath.

Once you've got the practice down you can color breath any time any where. You can color breath while standing, walking, driving, watching TV, listening to the radio, reading the paper, etc. The beauty of breathing color is it can be used to rejuvenate and restore balance anytime of the day - and it's free!

The next question, most of you are probably already asking, is what color do I breathe for what circumstance? You usually can't go wrong with white. It's an all-purpose color. After all, it's seven colors in one.

Beyond white, remember that red, orange and yellow are the stimulators, activators and energizers. At the upper end of the spectrum blue, indigo and violet are the relaxers, healers and purifiers. Green, in the middle of the spectrum, promotes peace, harmony and serenity.

The following are lists of keywords to assist you in selecting an appropriate color

Red   Action, vim, vigor, extroversion, initiator, pioneer, stimulator, etc.

Orange   Enthusiasm, cheerful, exurberance, optimism, ambitious, vitality, etc.

Yellow   Circulation, mental activity, speech, communication, creativity, etc.

Green   Quiets, refreshes, nourishes, prosperity, stablizer, restful, etc.

Blue   Tranquil, soothes, cools, introspective, relaxed, etc.

Indigo Purifies, intuition, justice, compassion, sensitive, understanding, etc.

Violet Calms, spiritual, transmutes, inspires, meditative, beauty, etc.

Color breathing can also be used to assist and speed up the natural healing process. You can direct the color energy to the ailing body part by focusing your attention there as you continue rhythmic breathing.

It has been reported that the warmer colors, red, orange and yellow are useful in overcoming a cold. Blue has been used to lower a fever or reduce inflamation.

Browse for books on color in your local bookstore. Many go into the specifics of using color breathing and colors generally to assist the natural healing process.

Noetic mind perceives,
Consciousness receives
Knowledge of the way
To function day by day.

Joy currents descend,
Heart energies ascend;
Peace of mind,
Love of man-kind.

Impersonal will directs
Natural pattern erects;
Willingly fulfills the laws
And eliminates psychic flaws.

Light Wave 73

Chakra Color Balance

Interpenetrating the physical body is the energy body. The energy body is etheric, subtle; it is not a body you can see or put a finger on. It's vibrational structure is on a higher frequency than the physical body.

Awareness and recognition of the energy body is mandatory in order to stabilize Tuning to the Spiritual Frequencies. What happens in the energy body manifests in the physical body.

If your attention is focused on constructive, satisfying and positive thoughts, feelings and activities then the energy body is in an harmonious condition. On the other hand, if your attention flits without direction into destructive, unsatisfying and negative thoughts, feelings and activities then the energy body is in an inharmonious condition. Either way the physical body feels the effects.

Now, just as the physical body has major regulatory centers we call organs and glands, the energy body has major regulatory centers called chakras (wheels of energy in Hindu) or energy centers. Each of the seven major energy centers (see figure #8 on page 142) has an affinity with one of the seven major colors.

When you misdirect your energies through unconsciousness, ignorance, habit or selfishness then the chakras are instantaneously effected adversely. As a result, the energy colors in each chakra are less brilliant; the shades are darker, more unrefined.

In order to regenerate the energy centers, thus bringing back brilliant colors, you can do the chakra color balance. Refer to the chakra chart as a guide to location and color.

Sit comfortably where you will not be disturbed for at least twenty minutes. Hold the left hand, palm down, six to eight inches above the crown chakra. Take the thumb and first two fingers of the right hand, bring them together and place them lightly on the top of the head.

Next, visualize a vibrant violet light. Hold that vibrant violet in your mind's eyes as you breath as follows: one short rapid breath through the nose and exhale to the count of six through the mouth.

Continue the process for a few minutes. If your left arm gets a little tired, lower it for a few seconds. Relax it, then return it into position. Be sure to maintain the violet visualization and breathing.

After the crown chakra, move to the brow chakra in the center of the forehead. Repeat the process only this time visualize indigo. If you have difficulty visualizing the colors refer to your rainbow. Look at the appropriate color directly.

When you finish all seven chakras visualize white light. Take both hands, and hold them in front of your torso palms turned toward the body. Breathe naturally. Now pass your hands alternately from the lower torso to the upper torso about fifty times. Continue visualizing the white light.

Treasure the light,
Stand and fight;
Cast out negative mood,
Starve it, no light-food.

Guard the precious flame,
Stake your cosmic claim;
Mine fire from fire,
Each breath inspire.

Protect the inner star,
Burn away the scar;
Raise fire to the field
Apocalypse unsealed.

Light Wave 74

Rainbow Meditation

There are literally hundreds if not thousands of different meditation practices. You may meditate regularly using a method that works well for you. You may not meditate at all or only occasionally.

Before I introduce you to the rainbow meditation which utilizes the seven spectrum colors, I want to give some explanation of meditation.

The word meditation begins with med -which refers to medium, middle, the center. The suffix "ation" means expressing action. Meditation can be defined as actively coming to your center.

Meditation is not fantisizing, daydreaming, sleeping, dreaming or thinking. Meditation is a process whereby will and awareness work together to calm the incessant rise and fall of thoughts, words, images, feelings, desires, etc.

By whatever meditation method you use to reach "your center", "the silence", "the Buddha nature", "the spiritual frequencies", some wonderful changes occur. As a result of meditation you become more aware, more emotionally stable, more perceptive, more patient, more understanding - the list goes on and on.

When a person reaches the meditative state, a strengthing force comes over them gently and warmly. You become hermetically sealed. The inner-outer are one. Everything is the way it's supposed to be.

Although the rainbow meditation requires, especially at first, a quiet place, meditation does not necessarily require aloneness, peace and quiet.

In fact, many advanced schools of meditation emphasize applying meditation practices to every day activities like driving, washing dishes, working in the garden, talking - you name it you can apply meditation to it.

The Rainbow Meditation goes like this. Find a quiet, comfortable place to sit,preferably on a chair that does not have a lot of padding. You do not want to sink into the chair; you want to have solid support.

Now sit up straight, not rigidly, but relaxed. Eyes can be open or closed, whichever you prefer. You may want to try it both ways. Come to attention, be aware, concentrate.

Next, visualize a scintillating ball of white light just above your head. The ball of white light is alive, conscious. The white light begins radiating down through the top of your head, a shower of white light. See every cell of your brain, body and bones being bathed in the regenerating, revitalizing white light.

After you feel it a while, begin winding your way through the color spectrum from red to violet.

Now see the ball of white light transform into a brilliant, glowing globe of irradiant red. Feel the red energy raining its vibration force down through the top of the head. Feel the vital currents charging and recharging your cells. Feel wave after wave of red energy bathing your entire being.

When you feel enough red energy, move on to orange. See the red sphere transform into a glowing orange ball of light. Again, see the currents pour into you. Feel the orange light flow through every cell.

Continue the Rainbow Meditation from orange to yellow, green, blue, indigo, and violet. When you've completed the spectrum, conclude the meditation with the white light.

It's hard to say how long the Rainbow Meditation will take—probably between 10-30 minutes. You must be sensitive to the color energies. You'll discover that you will spend more time on some colors. It could be you're somewhat depleted in that color and require more in order to balance.

Notice how you feel after the Rainbow Meditation. Do you feel calmer, more relaxed, more aware, revitalized?

If you find the Rainbow Meditation too long requiring "stressful concentration" to keep going, stop. You don't have to push it. Work with the white light only until you feel like going through the color spectrum. Remember, the white light does contain all seven colors.

Another point to consider, what shade of red, what shade of orange, what shade of yellow, etc. is best for you to choose? I personally prefer the lighter shades, the pastels, which have more white. The more white, the more light - the frequency of the color is higher.

Experiment some with different shades. You'll find the color which suits you and benefits you the most.

Love knows only giving,
Wisdom practices living;
Will applies the power,
Balance the three each hour.

False love expects returns,
False wisdom book learns,
False will is selfish desire,
Unbalanced forces expire.

Give conscious love,
Wisdom comes from above,
Will is measured action,
Make whole the three-fold fraction.

Light Wave 75

Measuring Your Color Energies

In Chapter 13 you read about the spiraling ray of white light that enters the body at the top of the head. The white light differentiates into the seven spectrum colors manifesting through the seven major energy centers. See figure 8 on page 142.

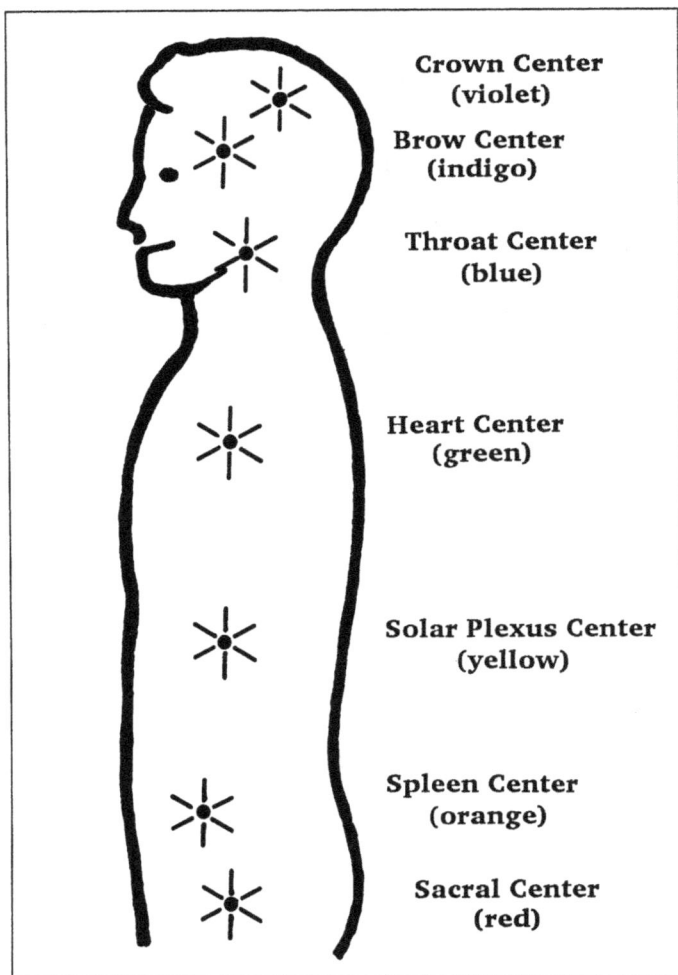

Figure 8: The Energy Centers

The energy centers radiate colored light which forms what is known as the aura. The aura energy field can be seen by clairvoyants as an egg-shaped force-field with many layers. The aura reader perceives the colors flowing and glowing in the aura and interprets their qualities.

For instance, if the aura reader sees a lot of pastel shades in the aura then he knows the person has a refined nature. On the other hand, if he sees a lot of muddy colors, dark reds, oranges and yellows, he knows the person is a brute with a powerfully selfish character.

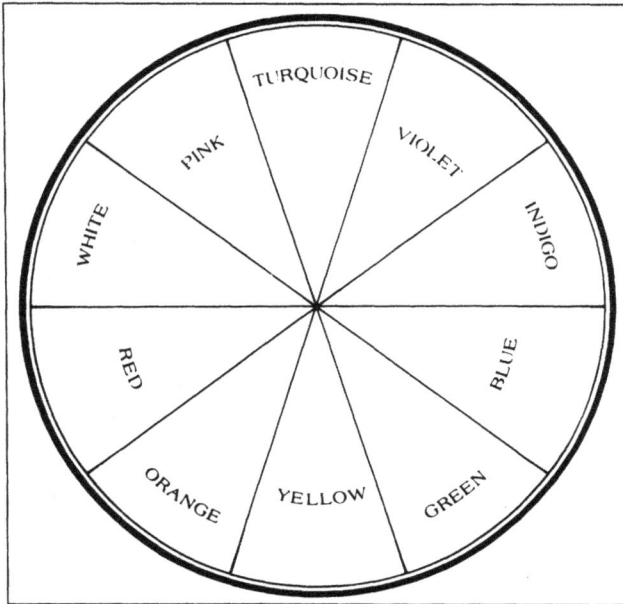

Figure 9: Pendulum Color Spectrum

I was fortunate to meet a fellow who does aura portraits. He spends two or three hours observing your aura while at the same time drawing what he sees. His skills as a professional artist makes his aura portraits come alive with expressive colors. He also spends time interpreting the portrait. He explains the different colors, layers, shapes and rays.

Some of the stories he tells about his insights as a kid are both interesting and humorous. He used to think everyone saw the way he did. As I recall one story, he was watching a concert and he saw a beautiful blue surrounding the musicians. At first he thought it was the stage lighting until he asked his friends if they saw the beautiful blue light. No, they did not see it. They thought he must be stoned.

There are numerous books which give step by step directions for developing auric sight. If you have an inclination you might want to buy a few books and learn to see the aura directly.

You can also feel the aura's color energies through a kind of inner vibrational touch. I use the pendulum, a dowsing tool, which is made from a weighted object on the end of a string or chain. The weighted object can be most anything from a crystal to a button. (See *Beyond Pendulum Power* by Greg Nielsen).

In the Pendulum Life Reading that I do, I measure a person's color energies using a pendulum and the Pendulum Color Spectrum. See figure #9 on page 143.

I proceed from color to color asking on a 0-10 scale how balanced is color *x* in so and so's auric-field? An eight, nine or ten reading tells me that color is vital, bright and circulating freely through the aura and chakras. A low reading, usually a six or below, indicates a need for a color or a low vibration of a color, a dark shade.

Through further questioning you often can pinpoint the source of the problem and then offer constructive suggestions for eliminating the problem. As a result, the balanced color energy can return.

On the Pendulum Color Spectrum I have included pink and turquoise. Pink falls in the upper end of the red spectrum and turquoise falls in between green and blue. I see these two colors playing leading roles in a lot of people's lives right now.

Pink is the color of universal love, and turquoise is the color of inventiveness. When you give without expectation of receiving, pink enters your auric-field. When you're highly original in your thinking, turquoise energies increase dramatically.

Summary

1. Light is energy vibrating at different wavelengths. In the visible light spectrum we see these energy wavelengths as color.
2. The shorter the wavelength the higher the frequency. The longer the wavelength the lower the frequency.
3. Becoming more color-conscious is an excellent way to enter into the energy world.
4. You can color breath anytime, anywhere. The beauty of breathing color is that it can be used to rejuvenate and restore balance.
5. Red, orange and yellow are the stimulators, activators and energizers. Blue, indigo and violet are the relaxers, healers and purifiers. Green promotes peace, harmony and serenity.
6. Awareness and recognition of the energy body is mandatory in order to stablize Tuning to the Spiritual Frequencies.
7. Just as the physical body has major regulatory centers we call organs and glands, the energy body has major regulatory centers called chakras or energy centers.
8. Each of the seven major energy centers has an affinity with one of the seven major colors.
9. When you misdirect your energies through unconsciousness, ignorance, habit or selfishness, the chakras are instantaneously effected adversely.

10. In order to regenerate the energy centers, practice the chakra color balancing exercise.
11. Meditation can be defined as actively coming to your center.
12. Meditation is not fantasizing, daydreaming, sleeping, dreaming or thinking.
13. Meditation is a process whereby will and awareness work together to calm the incessant rise and fall of thoughts, words, images, feelings, desires, etc.
14. After meditation you become more aware, emotionally stable, more patient and understanding. You feel stronger, more sensitive and more accepting of what is.
15. Practice the Rainbow Meditation. You'll feel calmer, more relaxed, revitalized.
16. The energy centers radiate colored light forming what is know as the aura.
17. You can measure color energies in many ways. Two ways are clairvoyant perception of the auric-field and an inner vibrational touch of the auric-field.

Chapter 16

The Science of Symbols

What A Symbol Is And Is Not

Many points in this chapter overlap and approach from a different angle many points taken up in Chapter 11, The Science of Semantics. Some people may react by thinking I'm being redundant. I can appreciate their point of view.

I make a distinction between redundancy and repetition. To me redundancy is repetition without purpose. Redundancy with purpose is beneficial repetition.

For one interested in a spiritual path, Tuning to the Spiritual Frequencies in a stable way, while still accepting and handling the responsibilities of everyday living, requires an awareness of how symbols affect you.

What is a symbol? A symbol represents a person, place or thing. A person's name is a symbol representing that person. If you write or say John with a particular John in mind then the symbol John is a useful communication tool.

Just think, you can write John a letter or call him anywhere in the world because you know his name, address and phone number. John's address and phone number are symbols representing a particular place, John's place.

Imagine yourself for a moment on a planet without names, person symbols, addresses and phone numbers, place symbols. You grow up with mom, dad, brother and sister. Of course, you have no word symbols mom, dad, brother and sister.

One day you're out walking with your "dad" and "brother". You see a "mountain lion" charging them from behind. Since you have no word symbols for "dad" and "brother" you have no language. Okay, so you have some grunts, groans, screams and crys, but they're not very specific.

You cannot yell "dad" and "brother" or their proper names. You scream, wanting to protect "dad" and "brother". It's a similar scream used for a dozen other purposes. "Dad" and "brother" are attacked by the man eating lion and killed.

A world without symbols would of course have little if any civilization. Science, art, music, dance, architecture, etc. could exist by demonstration alone. Without symbols the culture would not extend much beyond the family and tribe. The learning possibilities would be limited.

A symbol is useful only when it accurately represents a person, place or thing. Let's say our John X is at a football game with 50,000 other fans. There's an emergency at home. John's wife calls the stadium. The stadium announcer gets the message and announces, "Will John please call his wife at home".

Picture the scene. It is both humorous and tragic. How many Johns do you figure are sitting in the stands? How many football players on the field are named John.

There would be confusion, frustration, anger, fear, exasparation, etc. You might see a few thousand Johns run to the limited pay phones to call home. Maybe the star quarterback is a John. He loses his concentration resulting in an interception that loses the game.

A sound, image or written word that does not have a specific representation is meaningless, a noise. It is not a symbol.

If the stadium announcer asked John W. Phillips of 1720 Front Road to call his wife at home then chances are only one John would have gone to a pay phone.

When the rapids rush
And noise drowns the hush;
Hold steady to the path
To escape chaos wrath.

When earthly wants clamor
And spiritual ways stammer;
Remember the light,
It ends the fight.

When energies are drained
By multiplicity strained;
Quiet the chitter-chatter
Listen to the pitter-patter.

Light Wave 76

Multiordinality And Context

What does this mean: X? Did some answer pop into your head? Before I answer the first question let's explore the world of X and see what we find.

X is the 24th letter in the English alphabet. It's a consonant and it represents the sound eks like in box.

Before people could write, X was accepted as a legal signature. A person would make their mark differently than anyone else.

X can symbolize an unknown factor, variable, person, place or thing! The mathematical discipline algebra uses the X as an unknown in equations.

Have you ever made a small error writing out a check or filling out a bank deposit? Sometimes if the error is not too glaring you can X it out and make the change.

When you go into the voting booth you must X in the box to cast your vote. The X in this instance clearly indicates your choice. It represents a known not an unknown.

During ancient Roman times the X symbolized our 10. To the early Christian the X symbolized the Christ or a Christian, a believer in Christ.

Especially around Valentines Day you find X's on cards and candy. Each X indicates a kiss.

Back to math again. 8 X 8 = 64; the X means multiplication.

3" X 4" translated stands for 3 inches wide by 4 inches high. This shows dimension.

Those who enjoy astronomy and photography see the X used to show magnification, for example, 50X

X can also be a symbol for danger like at a railroad crossing or a poison warning.

Now let me ask, "What does this mean? X"? It's not so easy to answer is it? The answer that popped into your head before may not be the right one.

So what is the right answer? Congratulations to you if you said, "there is no answer" or "the question is meaningless" or some variation.

In fact, every symbol, every word, every image is multiordinal. Multiordinal simply means that a symbol has many, many meanings. Each specific meaning arises out of the context in which the symbol is used.

Off the top of my head I came up with 13 different contexts in which the symbol X is used differently. I'm sure there are many more than 13. Other contexts are coming to mind even as I write. In addition, each of the 13 I did sight have many shades of meaning depending on specific context.

Therefore, every symbol is multiordinal and derives its meaning from a context. A symbol without a context is meaningless. To automatically and unconsciously assign meaning to a symbol without a context leads to illusion, delusion, confusion.

If you harbor the false-to-fact belief that every symbol has a meaning then you will project a meaning into the symbol with ambiguous behavior the result. You can spend years on a so-called spiritual path pursuing nothing where you believe faithfully there is something.

Every few years we see in the news a so-called spiritual leader who is exposed for what he is - the blind leading the blind. He peddles symbols without context. He gives them meaning then convinces others to believe his meaning.

You will not go very far Tuning to the Spiritual Frequencies if you use symbols rigidly. You must remember that the symbols you feel comfortable with may be meaningless, have an entirely different meaning or mean almost the opposite to another.

Dogmas, creeds, faiths, beliefs, mind-sets, etc. tend to be convenient reified symbol systems. Presenting the possibility of multiordinality and context to someone with a reified one-valued orientation can be a mind opener. Many will fight, even die for nothing, for a meaningless symbol, for what they "believe in".

Energy vibrations
Infinite gradations;
Matter is alive,
Atoms, like bees in a hive.

Energy radiations,
Conscious sensations;
Psychic forces,
Must be bridled like horses.

Lightergy fire.
Spiritual tuning inspire;
Noetic ascension
Like a butterfly's resurrection.

Light Wave 77

Images And Words

On the non-symbol (energy world) level, images and words do not exist.

The energy world has to do with energy structures, functions, orders and processes. Symbols, images and words, are not the persons, places or things they represent.

You must understand the difference between energy, vibration, frequency, force, etc. and images, words, concepts, thoughts, etc. The symbol is not the energy structure on the non-symbol level.

Our culture places a lot of importance, gives a lot of value to the ability to form, remember, think, speak, and write symbols. As language comes alive in small children, we offer encouragement, give praise, show enthusiasm for a child's ability to speak, to use word symbols. Naturally, the child gets the clear impression that symbolizing is highly respected and rewarded.

When the children go to school they master their abc's and 1,2,3's and learn to read, write, add and substract. Children are taught how to use images and words. But are they taught about the non-symbol world, the energy world?

Do you recall any teacher throughout your days in school introducing you to and emphasizing the silent, non-verbal energy levels? No, I can't either. Yes, images and words are wonderful tools especially when they accurately reflect reality (patterns of energy in relationship). But to focus our educational process almost exclusively on symbols gradually detunes our children from the spontaneous sensitivity to energies and vibrations.

We need to compliment the symbol skills with non-symbol skills. Children, teenagers and adults must be instructed in perception, consciousness of abstracting, awareness, attention, visualization without fixation, concentration, attention without tension and focused relaxation. Greater value must be placed on these non-symbol skills if our educational system and, in turn, our civilization is to survive.

Why should non-symbol skills be valued so much? Because awareness brings your attention into the here-now. Awareness raises your energy. Awareness warns you about environmental dangers. Awareness reveals new possibilities. Awareness makes learning more enjoyable. Awareness increases understanding. Awareness promotes flexibility. Awareness integrates mind-body-spirit. Awareness assists you in thinking for yourself, etc., etc.

If non-symbol skills have so many benefits, why are they almost completely ignored? Whoever controls the symbols has the power. If the powerful discourage perceptive awareness they remain in power. When too many people become aware the powerful lose their power. Their symbols become meaningless.

We are bombarded with symbols from television, radio, newspapers, magazines, etc. day in and day out. A person without non-symbol skills is completely at the mercy of the incessant stream of symbols. A person's reason, will and judgement are forfeited.

A person has no choice at that point. They must buy; they must believe; they must vote; they must be unconscious; they must be a slave to things, etc.

The cosmic process is all in all,
You cannot walk before you crawl;
I this and I that,
A diet of I's makes us fat.

Consciously cooperate,
Fulfill your functional fate;
Work according to the plan,
Each child, woman and man.

Face the facts squarely,
They will judge you fairly;
The truth shall set you free,
Try it once or twice, you'll see.

Light Wave 78

Symbolitis

The symbol bombardment is so intense that most people are helpless when it comes to deciding what symbols are meaningful and which are meaningless. A high percentage of the population identify with any symbol without critical thought. A kind of mass hypnosis and hysteria is going on constantly through the mass media generated by the symbol-barons in politics, business and religion.

The mass hypnosis and hysteria for symbols let's call symbolitis. Symbolitis is a dis-ease, a dis-order, a de-structuring of the consciousness. A continuous stream of symbols, mostly meaningless, holds the mass attention. The individual consciousness, awareness, perception is eclipsed. A person's mind becomes completely mesmerized by the symbol stream, symbolitis.

What happens to someone with symbolitis? In three different ways, symbolitis manifests:
1. Blind adherance to authority.
2. Seeing everything in black and white.
3. One-dimensional dogmatism.

A person with symbolitis may behave in one, two or all three ways.

Let's take each symbolitis behavior and discuss it further.

When a person identifies with a political, business or religious leader and then indiscriminately agrees with everything they say or do, that person is suffering from Symbolitis 1. There's a tendency to set the prominent leader up as a god and then follow blindly. Dictators especially promote Symbolitis 1. Without Symbolitis 1, Hitler would have been a nobody.

Symbolitis 2, seeing everything in terms of black and white, occupies the mind in a futile conflict between right-wrong, good-bad, positive-negative, etc. It's a futile conflict because the person usually does not take the time or make an effort to gather the facts. Instead, they express an automatic opinion based on past symbol conditioning. A person with Symbolitis 2 is not aware that the opinion they express they have been conditioned to express.

One-dimensional dogmatism, Symbolitis 3, is symbolitis at its worst. A person's consciousness has crystalized into stone-cold unconsciousness. Why be aware of anything when everything is all figured out?

People with Symbolitis 3 are extremely dangerous to themselves and to others. They are so rigidly positive they are right that they will go against the facts.

I recently watched a news report about a devastating hurricane that struck the Texas Gulf Coast in 1969. Hundreds of people died, many needlessly because they suffered from a case of Symbolitis 3.

Despite the warnings, despite the evacuation orders some people stayed in the hurricane's path and held hurricane parties. Symbolitis 3 cost many hurricane partiers their lives.

How can one cure symbolitis? Scientific thinking is the antidote.

What exactly is scientific thinking? Scientific thinking is thinking from the facts, which are non-symbol energy structures. A 200-mile per hour hurricane is not a symbol. If you treat it as a symbol your chances of survival diminish. A hurricane is a non-symbol energy structure which does not change course because you're a nice person.

You do not have to be a scientist to think scientifically. Most anyone can learn to think from the facts and as a result eliminate the ravages of symbolitis.

One who thinks scientifically listens to authorities and observes what they do. If there is a big difference between what they say and what they do, scientific thinkers are alerted.

A scientific thinker knows by gathering facts that there are more than two ways to see anything. They see a wide range of shades between black and white. Right and wrong, good and bad, positive and negative disappear. The scientific thinker is then left with several choices, some more or less wise depending on present circumstances.

Planetary shield,
Star fire field;
Thru vacuum-fullness,
Light cell consciousness.

Galactic spiral,
Angelic smile;
Illumined souls
Living on gravity knolls.

Creations white light,
Snowflakes falling bright;
Brilliantly garbed archons
Compassionately harken.

Light Wave 79

Spiritual Static

Have you ever noticed the continuous, often incessant, flow of images and words through the mind? Those of you who meditate I'm sure are aware of the automatic and spontaneous rise and fall of symbols in the mind. Those of you who are not conscious of the steady flow of symbols through the mind take note.

Take five minutes out of your day today. That's all, just five short minutes. I guarantee those 300 seconds will be well worth it.

Find a quiet time. Sit comfortably. Now observe your thoughts. Be totally attentive to what you are thinking and imagining. Do you notice the thoughts enter your mental field, stay a while and then leave? Are you conscious of that process? Or do you slip into unconsciousness and forget what you were just thinking about?

If you drive a car, I'm sure you've had this experience. You drive a certain route day after day after day. You know it like the back of your hand.

Sometimes you can get into the car and next thing you know you have arrived. Driving the short trip you have drifted off, daydreaming, thought about something, but you couldn't remember what.

Tuning to the Spiritual Frequencies requires that you become conscious of the rise and fall of symbols through the mental field. Becoming conscious of the symbol stream tends to slow it down some and give you a detached feeling from the symbols.

Have you ever tuned in your favorite radio station and heard bursts of static interferring with clear reception? We all have, and it can be annoying. We lose part of the announcer's message or the song is impossible to enjoy.

During a thunder or electrical storm the static on your favorite radio frequency is particularly intense. When you think a lot, when you think too much, it's kind of like an electrical storm in the mind. Just like lightning disturbs the clear reception of radio frequencies, automatic thinking disturbs the clear reception of spiritual frequencies. Thinking, especially unconscious thinking, is spiritual static.

Let me put it plainly. If you think a lot, if you idolize thought, if you unconsciously daydream, etc., you are blocking the clear reception of spiritual frequencies. Tuning to the Spiritual Frequencies requires peace of mind.

How can you achieve peace of mind, which implies emotional calm and physical repose?

There are three structured and functional steps to peace of mind, the reduction of spiritual static. There are many methods by which you can take the three steps, but the three steps must be taken to achieve peace of mind.

Step One   Self-remembering. If you are identified with your thoughts then you are unconscious. When you remember to be conscious, you self-remember and you become aware that you are thinking.

Step Two   Self-observation. Once you self-remember you must self-observe. You begin the process of getting to know yourself. As you observe the symbol stream through your mental field you will notice patterns of thought. You will begin the process of not identifying with certain thoughts. Eventually, certain thought patterns will be eliminated reducing spiritual static.

Step Three   Bare attention. Bare attention is a state of wordless awareness. You look without association. You are the seer. A kind of detached force-field, a neutral energy enters your auric field when you go into bare attention. Your reception of the spiritual frequencies is continuous and crystal clear.

Take these three steps. Try it for a few days. You will breathe easier.

Gnostic Evolution,
Conscious Revolution;
Whirling Spiral Process,
Archetypal forces impress.

Once you touch the light,
It's Love-Wisdom-Might;
A cosmic battle is waged,
The elementals are enraged.

Demons, tricksters and imps,
Thought-emotion pimps;
Work every foible and fault
Till you wake up and put a halt.

Light Wave 80

Symbol Discrimination

Those in power, the politicians, the bankers, the lawyers, the doctors, the clergyman, etc., attain and maintain their power by using symbols. Take words and images away from the power brokers and where would they be? They would be powerless in the context of our present civilization.

The truth is we need symbols to operate civilization. Symbols in the form of language speed up communications. As a result, we learn more quickly and more efficiently.

Without language we would have to start all over again being the first human beings. With each human being starting from scratch our potential evolution would be limited. Food and shelter would probably be our only concerns.

For a civilization, a culture to thrive we need symbols. There is no way to get around that fact. The question is then how are those symbols going to be used and who is going to control the symbols?

For a civilization to survive, for a person to survive, for you to survive, the symbols that are used must accurately stand for something.

For instance, let's say you're driving on a winding mountain road. Ahead you see a sign indicating a sharp curve to the right, reduce speed to twenty miles per hour (see figure #10 below on this page). You identify with the symbol. You automatically believe it's accurate.

As you approach the curve you reduce your speed. You see the curve. You brake slightly. You turn the steering wheel to the right. You're in the curve; you're out of the curve.

Figure 10: Road Sign *Curve Right*   Figure 11: Road Sign *Curve Left*

You do not think much of it but in some small way you appreciate the accurate symbol, the road sign. In bad weather, in a rain storm or in a snow storm, you would appreciate it even more.

Let's view another scenario. Look at the sign in figure #11 on page 155. This sign indicates the road curves to the left instead of the right. Perhaps the highway crew mistakenly pulled the wrong sign (symbol) out. Or, even worse, a crew member was deranged and knowingly pulled the sign out fully expecting others would drive off the mountain to their deaths.

Now, as you approach the curve, you reduce your speed anticipating a curve to the left. You see the curve. You're surprised, shocked, panic stricken, terrified. It's hard to predict what your emotional reaction will be. You brake hard. The car goes into a skid. You stop at the edge of the cliff. You almost died. In bad weather you would have plunged to your death.

To survive, the symbols used must stand for something. Now do you see what I mean? There are a lot of people in powerful positions who intentionally use symbols to steer people in the wrong direction. Watch out. Be careful. Check things out for yourself.

The power brokers maintain their power as long as a sufficient number of people believe their symbols accurately stand for something. When a power broker betrays that trust and uses symbols for excess profits and fame, thousands, even millions of people suffer, sometimes even die.

Was the oil shortage in the mid 1970's fact or fiction? The oil barons produced an oil shortage and made billions. Are the Jews innately evil, true or false? Hitler enforces a lie putting six million Jews to their death.

Tuning to the Spiritual Frequencies requires symbol discrimination. You must not automatically and unconsciously attribute meaning to a symbol. You must discriminate whether or not it has validity.

Habitual identification with meaningless symbols leads to unconsciousness, lowered vitality, sickness, frustration, pain, suffering and death. You must recognize and accept the fact that their are people blinded and intoxicated by their power. The power hungry, the power drunk, the powerful know how to maintain or increase their power base by portraying lies as truth. **BE AWARE!**

Summary

1. For one interested in Tuning to the Spiritual Frequencies in a stable way coming to grips with symbols is a must.
2. What is a symbol? A symbol represents a person, place or thing. A person's name is a symbol representing that person.
3. A symbol is useful only when it accurately represents a person, place or thing.
4. Every symbol, every word, every image is multiordinal! Multiordinal simply means that a symbol has many meanings. Each specific meaning arises out of the context.

Tuning to the Spiritual Frequencies

5. A symbol without a context is meaningless. To automatically assign meaning to a symbol without a context leads to illusion, delusion, confusion.

6. You can spend years on a so-called spiritual path pursuing nothing where you believed faithfully there was something. Many will fight, even die for nothing, for meaningless symbols, for what they believed in.

7. You must understand the difference between energy, vibration, frequency, force, etc. and images, words, concepts, thoughts, etc. The symbol is not the energy structure on the non-symbol level.

8. To focus our educational process almost exclusively on symbols gradually detunes our children from the spontaneous sensitivity to energies and vibrations.

9. Greater value must be placed on non-symbol skills if our educational system and, in turn, our civilization is to survive.

10. A person without non-symbol skills is completely at the mercy of the incessant stream of symbols. A person's reason, will and judgement are forfeited.

11. The symbol bombardment through the mass media is so intense that most people are helpless when it comes to deciding which symbols are meaningful and which are meaningless.

12. Symbol hypnosis and hysteria is symbolitis. Symbolitis is a disease, a dis-order, a destructuring of consciousness.

13. Symbolitis leads to: 1) blind adhering to authority, 2) seeing everything in black or white and 3) one-dimensional dogmatism.

14. Scientific thinking cures symbolitis. Scientific thinking is thinking from the facts, which are non-symbol energy structures.

15. Tuning to the Spiritual Frequencies requires that you become conscious of the rise and fall of symbols through/in the mental field.

16. Just like lightning disturbs the clear reception of radio frequencies, automatic thinking disturbs the clear reception of spiritual frequencies. Thinking, especially unconscious thinking, is spiritual static.

17. There are three steps to the reduction of spiritual static: 1) self-remembering, 2) self-observation and 3) bare attention.

18. For civilization to survive, for a person to survive, for you to survive, the symbols that are used must accurately stand for something.

19. Tuning to the Spiritual Frequencies requires symbol discrimination. You must not automatically and unconsciously attribute meaning to a symbol. You must discriminate whether or not it has validity.

20. Habitual identification with meaningless symbols leads to unconsciousness, lowered vitality, sickness, frustration, pain, suffering and death.

Chapter 17

The Science of Synthesis

What Is Synthesis?

The Blindmen And The Elephant
by John Godfrey Saxe

It was six men of Indostan
To learning much inclined,
Who went to see the elephant
(though all of them were blind),
That each by observation
Might satisfy his mind.

The first approached the elephant,
And happening to fall
Against his broad and sturdy side,
At once began to bawl:
"God bless me! But the elephant
Is very like a wall!"

The second, feeling of the tusk,
Cried, "Ho! What have we here
So very round and smooth and sharp?
To me 'tis mighty clear
This wonder of an elephant
Is very like a spear!"

The third approached the animal,
And happening to take
The squirming trunk within his hands,
Thus boldly up and spake:
"I see," quoth he, The elephant
Is very like a snake!"

The fourth reached out an eager hand,
And felt about the knee:
"What must this wondrous beast be like
Is mighty plain" quoth he:
"'Tis clear enough the elephant
Is very like a tree!"

The fifth, who chanced to touch the ear,
Said:"E'en the blindest man
Can tell what this resembles most;
Deny the fact who can,
This marvel of an elephant
Is very like a fan!"

The sixth no sooner had begun
About the beast to grope.
Then, seizing on the swinging tail
That fell within his scope,
"I see," quoth he, "The elephant
Is very like a rope!"

And so the men of Industan
Disputed, loud and long,
Each in his own opinion
Exceeding stiff and strong.
Though each was partly in the right
They all were in the wrong!

Synthesis is a combining of parts to make a greater whole. The elephant is a living organic synthesis. As the poem so clearly illustrates, it is you and I who divide and separate what cannot be divided and separated.

The whole is, indeed, greater than the sum of the parts. When we analyze, focus on the parts, without synthesizing we are like the blindmen groping in the dark. Every person, place and thing is a synthesis, a whole interconnected to a greater whole.

Tuning to the Spiritual Frequencies is a synthesizing process. Thinking about anything, even Tuning to the Spiritual Frequencies, is an analytical process. Analysis blinds; synthesis binds.

If you are not that familiar with synthesis, don't feel left out. For the most part, our cultural system, especially the educational system, does not encourage synthesis skills. Analysis and specialization are encouraged. Synthesis and eclectic learning are discouraged.

In the next few pages, I will outline several methods by which you can apply synthesis to your life. If you apply these methods you will discover a new world, you will see where you never saw before and you will increase your choices a thousandfold.

The Alchemists have sung,
"The gold is in the dung";
The light is in the dark,
Transmutation builds the ark.

Earth, water, fire, air
Scattered here and there;
Mix, blend and boil,
Becomes the anointing oil.

Mercury, Moon, Sun,
Planet-forces spun
Into the Robe of Glory,
The start of another story.

Light Wave 81

Combinations And Permutations

How can you use synthesis in a practical everyday way? When you look at the combinations and permutations of any life situation you are using synthesis to discover the possible choices or alternatives. The more factors involved the more choices.

To see your choices you must combine and permutate factors, synthesis. The following is a formula for determining your choices in any life situation.

Synthesis Formula

Factors/Life Facts
1. X
2. Y
3. Z
4. A
5. B
   Etc.

Choices
1. XY
2. XZ
3. XA
4. XB
5. YZ
6. YA
7. YB
8. ZA
9. ZB
10. AB
  Etc.

Notice factors/life facts increase one by one. By combining the five factors/life facts there are ten choices. Obviously, then, the more factors involved in a life situation the more choices with which you are confronted.

Now, when it comes to using the synthesis formula you simply replace the algebraic symbols X, Y, Z, A, B, etc. with life facts. Let's take a few examples and see what happens.

Example #1: Summer Vacation Destinations

Factors/Life Facts
1. X = Grand Teton Mts.
2. Y = Monterey
3. Z = Disneyland

Choices
1. X = Grand Tetons
2. Y = Monterey
3. Z = Disneyland
4. XY = Tetons/Monterey
5. XZ = Tetons/Disneyland
6. YZ = Monterey/Disneyland
7. XYZ = Grand Tetons/Monterey/Disneyland

There are three destinations Sally and Rob have in mind for their summer vacation. Using the synthesis formula, there are seven possible choices for their summer vacation. Naturally, the choice they make will depend on other factors such as length of time, vacation budget, form of transportation, etc.

The synthesis formula is a beautiful tool because it clarifies your choices. Sally and Rob may have thought in terms of three choices, Grand Teton Mts., Monterey Bay, Disneyland. By looking at the permutations and combinations they more than doubled their destination choices.

Example #2: $100,000 Investment

Factors
- X = Real Estate
- Y = Stock Market
- Z = Precious Metals
- A = Bonds
- B = Certificates of Deposit
- Etc.

Choices
- X = Real Estate
- Y = Stocks
- Z = Precious Metals
- A = Bonds
- B = Certificates of Deposit
- XY = Real Estate/Stock Market
- XZ = Real Estate/Precious Metals
- XA = Real Estate/Bonds
- XB = Real Estate/Certificates of Deposit
- XZ = Real Estate/Precious Metals
- YA = Stock Market/Bonds
- YB = Stock Market/Certificates of Deposit
- ZA = Precious Metals/Bonds
- ZB = Precious Metals/Certificates of Deposit
- AB = Certificates of Deposit/Bonds
- Etc.

I have listed only five ways of investing the $100,000; there are many, many more. The combinations and permutations give at least 15 choices.

The synthesis formula when applied to specific life situations will counteract rigid thinking. Maybe our hypothetical $100,000 investor thought only real estate was a wise investment. Looking at an array of choices at least opens the door to new possibilities and perhaps better ways or combinations of investing $100,000.

Example #3: "Love Relationship"

Factors
- X = Marriage
- Y = Live Together
- Z = Continue Dating
- A = Break Up
- Etc.

Choices
- X = Marriage
- Y = Live Together
- Z = Continuing Dating
- A = Break Up

XY = Marriage/Live Together
XZ = Marriage/Date
XA = Marriage/Break Up
YZ = Live Together/Date
YA = Live Together/Break Up
ZA = Date/Break Up
Etc.

Do you see what happens when you start combining factors that you normally do not consider combining? You get combinations like XY, Marriage/Live Together. Marriage seems to automatically mean Live Together. XY implies another choice; Marriage/Not Live Together which may be an excellent choice under certain circumstances.

Play with the synthesis formula. The possibilities are limitless. New, creative and inventive choices spontaneously arise. The synthesis formula will change your belief system and broaden your awareness.

Love force flowing,
Energies glowing;
Universal love,
Symbolized by the dove.

Love: fruit of wisdom
Unifies the kingdom;
Transmutes base desire,
Ignites the cosmic fire.

Love heals karmic pain,
Makes the unsane sane;
Serves the God-plan
And the human clan.

Light Wave 82

Holographic Thinking

Three dimensional photography or holography is an excellent analog for synthesis thinking, thinking in wholes, holographic thinking.

Remember the elephant story. We all tend to think in parts and then believe we know the whole. As you saw with the six men who touched the elephant, identifying the part with the whole leads to miscalculations, false judgements and misconceptions.

Before giving functional steps to achieve holographic thinking, let's take a look at holography. See figure #12 on page 164.

To create a hologram, a three-dimensional photograph, you must start with a laser light. A laser produces light of a single frequency which shines in a narrow and precise beam. In contrast, a flashlight produces diffused light of many frequencies with a wide beam.

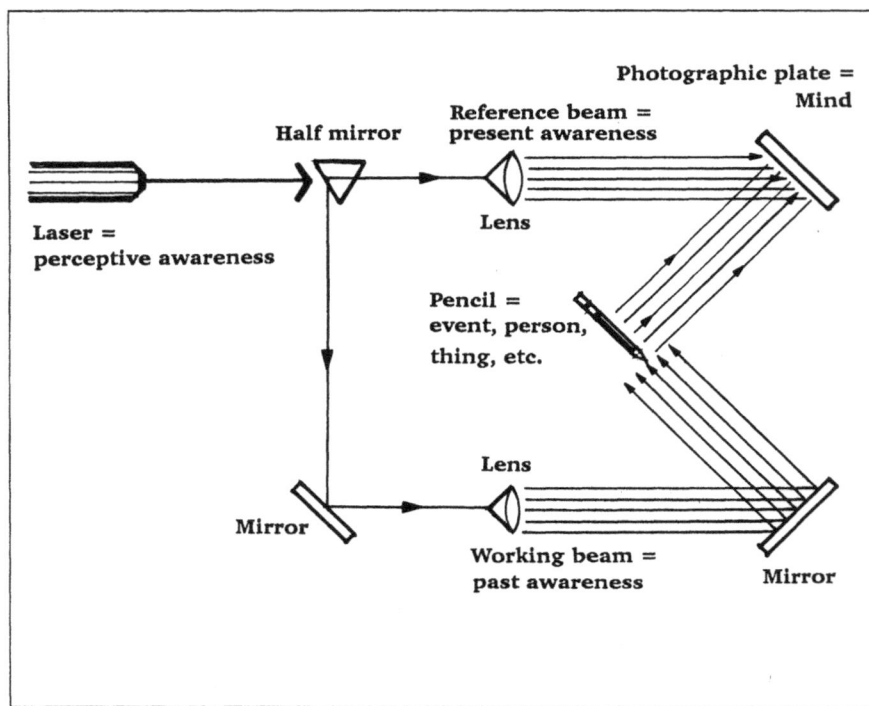

Figure 12: Holographic Thinking

In holography the laser light is directed through a semi-transparent mirror splitting the laser light in two. The reference beam continues on through the half mirror through a lens and spreads out onto a photographic plate. The other beam, the working beam, is reflected to a regular mirror, through a lens, spreads out and reflects off yet another mirror, illumines an object, and finally reflects off an object onto the same photographic plate as the reference beam.

The two beams interact in the photographic emulsion storing the laser lights experience with the object, a hologram. By illuminating the hologram with a laser light a three-dimensional image of the object appears suspended in midair looking very real.

Now, how can we correlate holography with synthesis thinking?

Laser Light= Perceptive Awareness
Reference Beam = Present Awareness
Working Beam = Past Awareness
Mirrors = Subconscious Memories
Lenses = Angles of Awareness
Object = Event, Person, Thing, Etc.
Photographic Plate = Mind

In order to have synthesis thinking or holographic thinking you must start with perceptive awareness. Perceptive awareness is keen and acute awareness which requires conscious effort in the present. Perceptive awareness is like laser light.

Automatic, semi-conscious awareness is like the diffused light from a flashlight. It illumines only part of the object, event or person. Automatic awareness is not focused keenly in the present. It associates automatically with the past. Remember the blindmen and the elephant again. They associate something from their past: wall, spear, snake, etc.

Once you're in a state of perceptive awareness you can see the event, person, thing clearly in the present (Reference Beam) which forms an accurate pattern in the screen of the mind (photographic plate). Seeing the event, person, thing from several different angles can be compared to the lens which focuses and spreads the laser light (Perceptive Awareness).

The working beam can be compared to your past perceptive awareness reflected and stored in your subconscious mind in the form of memories. The lens once again can be compared to many angles of perceptive awareness (experiences) in the past.

The past images are then reflected back to the conscious mind in the present (the photographic plate). The patterns in the present and past intermingle and form new patterns in the mind. (A synthesis thought, a holographic thought). Now you shine your perceptive awareness on that holographic thought and it will be an excellent representation of the actual event, person, or thing.

Holographic thinking creates holographic thoughts which are much more accurate image maps of reality. (Patterns of energy in relationship). The more accurate your maps the easier it is to plot a course. Naturally, you must always remember: the map is not the territory. Perceptive awareness is continuously required to make new holographic thoughts in order to make necessary life adjustments.

Love without wisdom is blind,
To things and people bind;
Personal love's embrace,
Karmic bonds encase.

Wisdom without love is cold,
Dull unpolished gold;
When the personality is first
The life is cursed.

When Love-Wisdom marry,
The Will forces quarry;
The mind-soul light
From the caves of midnight.

Light Wave 83

Psycho-Spiritual Synthesis

Say your name out loud. Do you hear yourself say your name? Guess what, that's not who you are. Your name is just a label, a way of communicating. It get's your attention; that's all.

You are vastly more than a verbal sound or a written word, your name! Structurally and functionally you have the capacity to experience instinctive, intellectual and intuitive forces.

1. Instinctive forces: Desire, emotion, anger, fear, fight, sex, hunger, survival, etc.
2. Intellectual forces: Words, images, thoughts, concepts, ideas, formulas, blueprints, plans, etc.
3. Intuitive forces: Hunches, feelings, dreams, imagination, creativity, inspiration, etc.

Centuries ago an alchemist wrote in his notebook, "We seem to have as many personalities as we have moods." He was and is so right. We are not a name; we are not one person. We are many persons. Like a diamond, we have many facets. The facets are all of our instinctive, intellectual and intuitive characteristics/personalities that combine (synthesize) to make us who we are.

Humpty Dumpty sat on the wall
Humpty Dumpty had a great fall
All the king's horses
And all the king's men
Could not put Humpty Dumpty
Back together again.

I'd like you to take a look at this nursery rhyme in a new light. Humpty Dumpty represents you or me. Before we are born, we are like Humpty Dumpty sitting on the wall. We are whole; we are on top of everything.

Then we are born into this world; Humpty Dumpty has a great fall! Our beautiful pristine world has come to an end. In a sense, we break into a thousand pieces like Humpty Dumpty does when he hits the ground.

As a new born baby, the young child, the teenager and the adult, we must learn how to survive. We have to get it together. In a sense, each eggshell fragment represents one of our facets, characteristics, personality traits.

The horses and the king's men could not put Humpty Dumpty back together again! If we're Humpty Dumpty who are the king's horses and men? They represent the social, political and economic institutions. A good education, marriage and a family cannot put you back together again. Being a voting Democrat or Republican will not put you back together again. Having a good job and earning a comfortable living will not put you back together again.

What, then, can put you back together again? The question should be who? The answer: You! You have to put yourself back together again. Money, social standing, higher education may assist you in your psycho-spiritual synthesis but you must make the decision and then persist in the self-knowledge and self-discovery process.

To gather your fragments and put yourself back together, again you must first see that you are not one but many. Seeing this requires that you go through the following:
1. Self-remembering
2. Self-observation
3. Self-knowledge

Self-remembering means becoming aware in the here-now. Self-observation simply means you observe your behavior, speech, thoughts, emotions, habits, images, attitudes, desires, etc. Self-knowledge is the natural result of long-term self-observation.

Now, once you achieve a certain degree of self-knowledge you stop identifying with some traits and characteristics which are in conflict with your purpose, plan and structure. You identify more with those functions which are in harmony with your purpose, plan and structure.

At that point, your individuality begins to emerge (your Humpty Dumptyness). You become much more than you were before when your personalities were warring - beliefs against desires, actions against words, feelings against thoughts, etc. The whole is greater than the sum of the parts.

Conscious currents of love,
Feelings from above;
Controls emotions boil,
Awakens the cosmic coil.

Feel-direct the love-glow
To pain and suffering below;
Past lives transformed,
Present life re-formed.

Love's regenerating force
Connects us to the source;
Merging with the one,
Melting into the sun.

Light Wave 84

The Alchemical Mixing Process

The medieval alchemists spent years mixing the four elements earth, water, fire and air in various proportions. Their goal was to produce the mysterious fifth element, the ether.

The ether was so sought after because it was the healing elixir, the fountain of youth, the aqua divinum, etc.

Most alchemists labored in the candlelight struggling to create the ether. Most failed. They were caught up in the literal mixing of strange element combinations.

There were a few master alchemists who discovered the crucible was truly their own psyche. The four elements were nothing more than the four primary psychological traits. The ether simply symbolized a psycho-spiritual synthesis, the four elements combined.

Now, let me clarify the psychological correspondence of each element.

Earth is the most stable element. It is not in constant motion like air, water and fire. At least not to the visible eye. A strong earth tendency usually manifests as determination, practicality and a willingness to work tirelessly to achieve material rewards.

Earth is reliable, steadfast, dependable, responsible. Earth sticks-to-it. Earth refuses to give up. Dreaming, fantasy, make believe - that's for the water and air parts of the psyche. The earth part wants to see, hear, taste, smell and touch reality.

Like everything else in the universe the elements have polarity, a positive and a negative. Too much earth can make a person rigid, fixed, dogmatic and habit-bound. A strong earth energy may make a person determined in the wrong direction. Hitting your head against a wall doesn't do anyone any good.

Other negative earth traits include status seeking, keeping up with the Joneses, making "things" more important than people, etc. In the final analysis earth is the structure, the container, the physiological organism.

Water is feeling, emotion, sensitivity and intuition. Water makes earth more pliable. Water turns the earth into a garden.

Water is in constant motion - the rise and fall of the ocean, the flowing river, evaporation and condensation. Water nourishes, feeds, preserves life. Water cleanses, purifies and washes away.

If you are kind, considerate, sympathetic, empathetic, imaginative, etc., then you probably have a lot of water energies. Negative water traits include dreaminess, hypersensitivity, moodiness, emotional attachment and possessiveness.

Air is mental activity and communication. Thinking, reasoning, speaking, analyzing, discussing are all air traits. Air is invisible to the naked eye and so are thoughts, ideas, words and images.

If you love to read, study, learn, exchange and share knowledge and information, air energies are prominent. On the negative side, air people can be too idealistic, impractical, all talk and no action and ineffectual intellectuals.

Fire is action. Do it; try it; experience it. If you don't know find out firsthand. Fire is adventure, exploration, courage and will. Fire excites, creates and warms things up.

Fire loves to lead, to be the pioneer, to go where no one has gone before. On the other hand, fire can leap before it looks, be the blind leader of the blind, burn itself out with too much activity.

An entire book could be written on the positives and negatives of the four elements. Here I've given you an idea, a feeling, an introduction.

When you consciously mix and combine the four elements, psychological traits, in yourself in a dynamic balanced way, you produce the ether, the fifth element. The ether represents a psycho-spiritual synthesis.

An individual who manifests the ether energies is magnetic, relaxed, articulate, functional, full of energy, respected, responsible, peaceful in adversity, ready to sprint into action, etc. In short, a person who has achieved the ether element, a balance of the psychological forces and energies, is in a position to consciously and continuously Tune to the Spiritual Frequencies.

Christ consciousness real,
Tune-listen-feel;
Overcomes the image-hold,
Transforms the psyche's mold.

Frequencies of light
Turn out the night;
Become the Light being,
Make the unseen seen.

Peaceful mighty power,
The dark ones cower;
The angels rejoice,
Hearing the Christ voice.

Light Wave 85

Becoming An Individual

Karen did everything right. She pleased her parents with straight A's from high school through college. She went on to graduate school and earned a Ph. D. in Psychology.

She married a medical doctor who was at the top of his class and tall, dark and handsome to boot. She set up a counseling practice that became highly successful.

Would you consider Karen an individual? Most people thought of Karen as a successful individual, an intelligent individual, a together individual.

Karen, on the other hand, did not think of herself or feel herself to be a together individual.

Karen felt that something was missing. She did not feel her psychological counseling was satisfying. She did not feel her marriage was satisfying. On the surface Karen had it all, underneath she had very little.

I want to make a clear distinction between personality and individuality. Personality has to do with the mask, how people see us superficially. Your personality becomes more prominent as your status increases. Status is usually the result of recognized achievement.

Individuality is much different than personality. Becoming an individual is an entirely different process. The first step in that process is seeing the personality for what it is: a mask, the role you play, your title, etc.

Karen was much more than a title, a write-up in *Who's Who*, a prominent psychologist. She felt something was wrong, but she couldn't put her finger on it.

Despite her apparent perfect life, Karen began to search for something more, something more meaningful. She set out on the path of becoming an individual.

An individual has gone through a process of recognizing personality for what it is - a lie; the illusion you are together when you are really broken and fragmented into a thousand pieces.

To become an individual (indivisible, undivided, whole) requires becoming conscious of each and every personality fragment. You stop identifying with the false personality that prides itself on being an individual and recognize the lack of inner togetherness. Now you can really know yourself. You see your faults clearly; you see your good points clearly.

As you get to know yourself more and more, you discover you have a certain structure with a certain purpose. What society, parents, teachers, etc. expected of you, wanted for you is often not what you are meant to do! Only you can get in touch with your true structure and purpose.

Karen had the courage to take the path from personality to individuality. As a result, her marriage dissolved; it never really existed! She could not counsel others in traditional socially accepted ways any more. She devoted much time and energy to knowing herself, to finding and feeling her true structure and purpose.

At the time of this writing, she has not stabilized as an individual, but she is well on her way. She is now sensing her structural purpose and discovering her plan. It is an exciting time as any "individual" will attest to.

The whole is, indeed, greater than the sum of the parts. In reality, the false personality is made up of many personalities. You become whole, an individual, by seeing your different personalities and choosing which will stay and which will leave.

Those personality fragments that must leave you stop identifying with. You stop feeding them energy. Without your identification, they have no energy. They cannot survive without energy.

Those constructive traits are then integrated around a consciousness that works with structures, functions and orders as fundamental. Slowly but surely that consciousness begins to work in harmony with the universe, the natural order. Eventually, that consciousness cannot work any other way but in harmony with the universe. An individual is born, radiating light and Tuned to the Spiritual Frequencies.

Summary

1. Synthesis is a combining of parts to make a greater whole.
2. When we analyze, focus on the parts without synthesizing, we are like blind men groping in the dark.
3. When you look at the combinations and permutations of any life situation you are using synthesis to discover the possible choices or alternatives.
4. The synthesis formula clarifies choices, counteracts rigid thinking and creates new possibilities.

5. To experience holographic thinking you must start with perceptive awareness. Perceptive awareness is keen, acute awareness requiring conscious effort. It is like laser light.
6. Patterns in the present and past intermingle and form new patterns in the mind, a synthesis thought, a holographic thought.
7. Shine your perceptive awareness on a holographic thought, and it will be an excellent representation of the actual event, person or thing.
8. You are vastly more than a verbal sound or a written word, your name! Structurally and functionally you have the capacity to experience instinctive, intellectual and intuitive forces.
9. You are not one person; you are many persons. Like a diamond you have many facets. The facets are all of your instinctive, intellectual and intuitive characteristics/personalities that combine (synthesize) to make you who you are.
10. To gather your fragments and put yourself back together again you must first see that you are not one but many. Seeing this requires that you go through the following: 1) Self-remembering 2) Self-observation and 3) Self-knowledge.
11. When your individuality begins to emerge you become much more than you were before when your personalities were warring - beliefs against desires, actions against words, feelings against thoughts, etc.
12. There were a few master alchemists who discovered the crucible was truly their own psyche. The four elements were nothing more than the four primary psychological traits. The ether symbolized a psycho-spiritual synthesis, the four elements combined.
13. An individual who manifests the ether energies is magnetic, relaxed, articulate, functional, full of energy, respected, responsible, peaceful in adversity, ready to spring into action, etc.
14. The personality has to do with the mask, how people see us superficially. Becoming an individual means you see the personality for what it is: a mask, the role you play, your title, etc.
15. As you become an individual your consciousness begins to work in harmony with the universe, the natural order. Eventually, your consciousness cannot work any other way than in harmony with the universe.
16. Eventually, you are born as an individual radiating light and Tuned to the Spiritual Frequencies. *You are greater than the sum of your parts.*

Chapter 18

The Science of Cosmology

What Is Cosmology?

On the face of it cosmology is simply the study of the cosmos. Cosmos in Greek means universe. So cosmology is the study of the the universe.

To take on the study of the universe may trigger feelings of intimidation, awe, wonder, excitement, adventure, etc. No doubt it may appear, at first, to be an impossible task.

Let me clarify something right away. By the "Science of Cosmology" I do not mean the study of the universe from a modern science point of view - physics, astrophysics, etc. Here the "Science of Cosmology" refers to all dimensions, worlds, levels of consciousness not just our four-dimensional space-time universe.

Traditional scientists use the five senses and extensions thereof, microscopes, telescopes, spectroscopes, to measure the structures of this space-time continuum. Their scientific measurements are made on essentially three levels within this four-dimensional corner of the cosmos: They are the 1) macroscopic - stars, space, planets, 2) microscopic - minerals, plants, animals, humans, and 3) submicroscopic - protons, electrons, neutrons.

For the most part, traditional scientists do not acknowledge or even consider extrasensory perception a valid and accurate means of measuring/experiencing the cosmos. There is no point in trying to convince, prove, show or explain that the human nervous system, the mind-brain, consciousness can experience this corner of the cosmos and every other corner of the cosmos.

There are indeed more than four dimensions, although it cannot be proven using the instruments of traditional science. It can, however, be experienced by a spiritual scientist learning to tune and Tuning to the Spiritual Frequencies.

Measuring instruments and machines do not have anywhere near the sensitivity that a conscious being has. A spiritual scientist leaves the instruments and machines behind. They are definitely useful up to a point. Beyond a certain point consciousness functioning in extrasensory perception experiences other dimensions, worlds and levels of consciousness.

Beyond the four-dimensional universe you enter the fifth dimension, the world of thought, feeling, emotion and desire... psychological forces, forms, fields and frequencies. The words "fifth dimension" sound a bit mysterious. The only mystery is the lack of awareness of thoughts, feelings, emotion and desire.

Psychology, metaphysics, occultism, psychism, parapsychology and mysticism focus mostly on the fifth dimension and, to some degree, its relation with four dimensions.

The study of cosmology goes beyond the fourth and fifth dimensions. Tuning to the Spiritual Frequencies begins in the sixth dimension, the world of light, love, wisdom, understanding, will...

Consciousness in and through human form has the potential of exploring the cosmos through direct perception and experience. Matter, energy, space, time, thought, feeling, emotion, desire, love, light, wisdom, understanding, will... the frequencies are limitless. The multi-dimensional cosmos is not merely a mental map or mathematical construct. It is living structures, functions and orders.

Circulating the light
Opens brilliant sight;
Dissolves psychic blocks,
Noetic consciousness knocks.

Feel swirling light,
Consciousness takes flight;
Shakes the body cells,
Exit the dark force hells.

Bathe in waterfall light,
Transforms weakness to might;
Centered in the flame,
The instincts forever tame.

Light Wave 86

A Cosmic Map

Where do you focus your attention? Wherever you focus your attention and identify, that's where you are in the cosmos. The more conscious you are of where you're focusing your attention the more freedom and free will you have to contact and experience different levels of cosmic consciousness.

Take a look at the cosmic map. See figure #13 on page 176.

Spiritual World

- Seven dimensions includes: the one presence, the one power, the one plan, the one process.
- Six dimensions includes: love, light, wisdom, understanding, will, etc. vibrations

Psychological World

- Five dimensions includes: thought, feeling, emotion, desire, vibrations

Physical World

- Four dimensions of space-time - seeing, hearing, touching, tasting, smelling, etc.

After reviewing the cosmic map, what percentage of your attention is focused in each level? If you're not sure, you might want to observe yourself over a few days and see. Again, where you focus your attention is where you are in the cosmos.

"How can that be?" "I'm always in my body." "How can I be somewhere else?" "How can I be in another dimension yet in my body?"

These are all valid questions. The answer hinges on the word "focus". Just because you're walking, working, eating, sleeping, etc. does not mean you're focused in the physical world, the world of the body and the five senses. Have you ever known anyone who you considered to be "spaced out"? They didn't hear a word you said; they forgot what they were supposed to do; they made a mess of things.

In fact, they were not focused in the physical body. Their attention randomly and unconsciously wandered indiscriminately in the psychic world of images, fantasies, thoughts, feelings, etc. In reality, the physical body operates on automatic pilot while consciousness more or less leaves the body. For a time, that person is, for all intents and purposes, "out of their body".

Tuning to the Spiritual Frequencies requires that you focus attention in the sixth and seventh dimensions. Does that sound "far out", "difficult", "hard", etc. ? It isn't. Meditation is nothing more than focusing attention and Tuning to the Spiritual Frequencies.

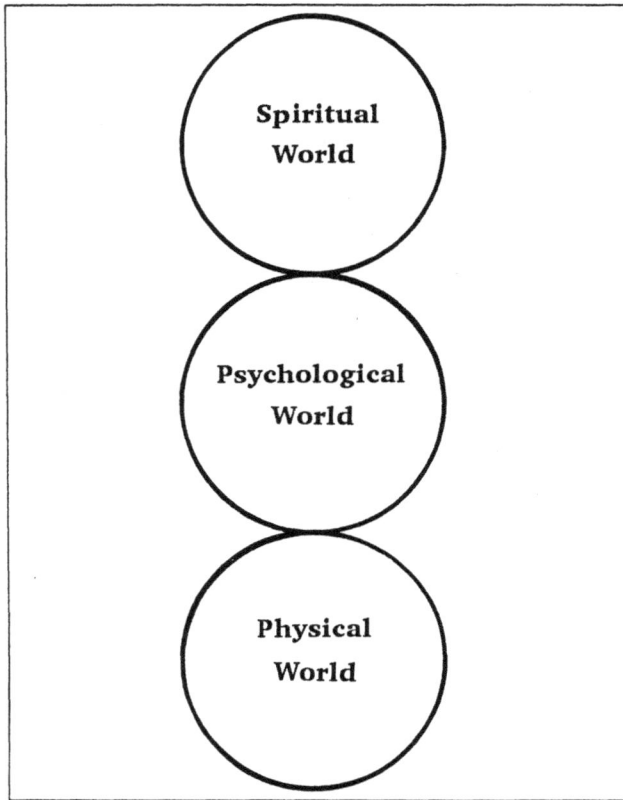

Figure 13: A Cosmic Map

True, if your attention wanders aimlessly and indiscriminately, you may have to go through a training period learning how to steady your attention. (See *Functional Mind Training* by Greg Nielsen.) With regular practice over a few weeks, months and years, you should be able to focus your attention at will. Naturally, the more practice, the steadier and longer you can hold your attention.

Eventually, your focusing ability will be so developed that you'll be able to focus on several levels at once. Multi-focuses will take place at the same time. You'll be able to monitor your different focuses, choosing major and minor focuses depending on current circumstances and needs.

The science of cosmology is not as abstract and philosophical as you might have thought. You are instrinsically and intimately integrated in the cosmic organism as a whole. Focus your attention and there you are. Hold your attention steady and you'll feel the vibrations of that dimension.

Tuning to the Spiritual Frequencies

You do not have to be an astronaut to explore the cosmos. You do not have to be a mystic, a yogi, or a shaman to experience the multi-dimensional cosmos. If you can focus your attention steady for a time, your journey has begun. You have entered the *playground of the gods.*

Plant the golden seed,
Grows deed by deed;
Burst through the shell,
It teems and swells.

Breaking the earth's crust,
Into the light world thrust;
Climbing through the air,
Spiraling stair by stair.

Then, the golden flower blooms,
It's petals, fluttering plumes;
With Light's beauty graced,
Of the Divine nectar taste.

Light Wave 87

Cosmic Structure

At this very moment, as you are reading this, Earth is whirling through space on its 365-day journey around the sun. Earth is a chunk of cosmic structure. It has a north pole and a south pole, positive and negative. Earth is a giant magnet orbiting the sun.

Everything in the cosmos has a positive and negative polarity. Galaxies, solar systems, stars, planets...atoms, molecules, cells...people, places, things. Look for yourself. Try to find anything that does not have polarity, positive-negative.

Work on finding something that does not have polarity. If you find it, the cosmos does not have structure. From the most mundane to the most sublime, polarity is the root structure of any unity.

When you gaze up in the night sky what do you see? Stars. Right. What else? Space. Right again. The star light and space dark, polarity.

Take a look at the book you're reading. Do you see the polarity? The content is positive/informative and the cover is negative/protective.

Now look at your hands. Yes, there's polarity there too!

Practice seeing cosmic structure, polarity in unity...the two in the one.

As you experience cosmic structure more and more I expect you will be changed forever. You will probably feel more integrated with the universe. Feelings of separateness will disappear or, at least, be reduced considerably.

We are all potential cosmologists. By becoming conscious of cosmic structure we begin the process of being an actual cosmologist. Your awareness of polarity in everything, everywhere will stir a force within. Wonder, awe, amazement, excitement, a craving for knowledge...you will want to explore the cosmos. Polarity in unity, the essence of cosmic structure, is your compass.

Polarity in unity is not just without; it is also within. Without/within, outer/inner...polarity again! There's the body part of you with all its polarities and there's the psychological part of you with all its polarities.

Polarity in Unity

Positive (+)	Negative (-)
Within	Without
Inner	Outer
Spiritual	Psychological
Mind	Body
Etc.	Etc.

Before I go on, let me clear up any possibility of an inaccurate semantic reaction. "Positive/Negative" have nothing to do with morality in the sense of good or bad, right or wrong. If the earth's north pole is good is the south pole bad?

In a psychological connotation of positive and negative, one person's positive can be another person's negative. For example, a race car driver speeding at 200 mph is positive, especially if he wins the race. If you speed down the interstate at 200 mph that's negative, especially if you end up in jail or dead.

To summarize, cosmic structure can be reduced to:

0 - No-thing
1 - Unity
2 - Polarity

What is the law of three?
Positive, negative polarity;
See this cosmic law
Operate in the all and all.

Practice the law of three,
Then no need to disagree;
Relating energy binds
Bodies, hearts and minds.

Apply the law of three,
Reveal the mystery;
Force, resistance, goal
Consciously become whole.

Light Wave 88

Archetypal Patterns

There are archetypal patterns throughout the cosmos. An archetype is an original pattern or prototype. The two archetypal patterns I want to tell you about are: 1) Geometric Archetypes and 2) Human Archetypes.

All forms in the cosmos can be reduced to two geometric archetypes: 1) The Circle and 2) The Triangle. The circle and the triangle are the mother and father of all forms. See figure #14 and #15 below on this page.

The following is a partial list of circle and triangle offspring. (A comprehensive book on geometry will give you a more complete list.)

Circle	Sphere
	Oval
	Spiral
	Cylinder
	Etc.
Triangle	Pyramid
	Square
	Rectangle
	Cube
	Etc.
Circle/Triangle	Cone

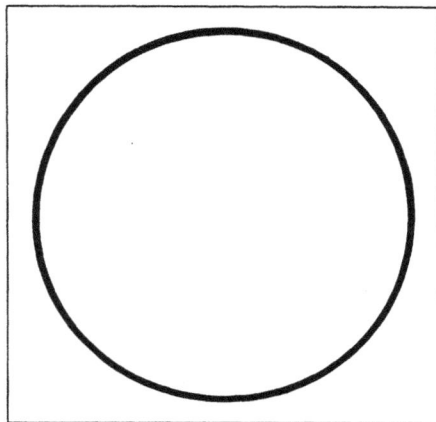

Figure 14: The Circle   Figure 15: The Triangle

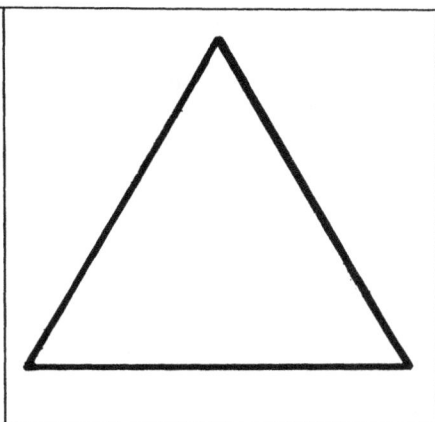

How do I know that every form in the cosmos can be reduced to the geometric archetypes: circle and triangle? For nearly two decades I have searched for anything, any manifest form that cannot be reduced to the circle and triangle. See if you find something!

Let's try a few things and see what happens. I'm going to look around me quickly and spontaneously choose three things and see their geometric archetypes: 1) coffee mug, 2) station wagon and 3) stapler.

I'm not going to observe the internal geometric patterns. That could take a whole chapter, especially the station wagon. I'll limit myself to the external shapes.

Visualize a coffee mug. Obviously we're dealing exclusively with the circle archetype. The mug that I'm looking at is a hollow cylinder approximately five inches high and three and one-half inches in diameter. On one side of the cylinder are two circular holes used for finger grips.

Visualize a station wagon. Many variations of the circle and triangle make the station wagon's external form. The wheels are circular. The overall body shape is a rounded or curved rectangle. The window shape has numerous triangular combinations. The gas cap is round. The mirror is rectangular. (A rectangle is a combination of at least two triangles.)

An automobile design engineer could give us the specific geometric terms. Look at a station wagon. Do you see any shapes other than circle and triangle combinations?

Visualize a stapler. It has an overall curved rectangular shape. The curved part reduced to a partial circle (semicircle) and the rectangular to interconnected triangles. I could go on, but I think I've made my point.

Practice looking at things and people geometrically. Your experience of archetypal patterns will tune you into the cosmos.

All human archetypes can also be reduced to two: *female* and *male*. Here are some of the variations:

Female		*Male*	
	Mother		Father
	Girl		Boy
	Sister		Brother
	Grandmother		Grandfather
	Aunt		Uncle
	Wife		Husband
	Niece		Nephew
	Granddaughter		Grandson

What I've just pointed out seems so obvious. Anybody can see the human race has two root forms female and male. Remember cosmic structure, polarity! In the next section you will discover why it's important to clearly define the human archetypes - female/male.

Give up your psychic force,
Return it to the source;
Offer it to the one,
The fiery descent has begun.

Will thought, emotion, desire
Toward the crown of fire;
Sacrifice automatic urge
Feel light waves surge.

Direct psychic force
Toward heaven's spiral course;
Incessant letting go,
Incandescent glow.

Light Wave 89

"As Above, So Below"

Ancient hermetic philosophers emphasized the axiom "as above, so below." What did they mean? The "as above" referred to the grand scheme of things and the "as below" referred to the human condition.

The hermetic philosophers, for example, divided the cosmos into three levels: Spiritual Light, Psychic Activity and Physical Manifestation (as above). In the human sphere (so below) the correspondence is: spiritual, psychological and physical.

From one point of view there is no above or below. If you're traveling through outer space, what's above and what's below? Above/below, up/down, higher/lower do not exist. In a very real sense everything, every person, every place is in the grand scheme of things.

Once you establish and maintain your Tuning to the Spiritual Frequencies, your perception changes. You begin to see-experience-feel that you live in one world, one multi-dimensional cosmos. The tendency to divide, separate life into a duality: spiritual/material, above/below, good/bad, etc. is replaced by a unified perception.

Whatever you look at reflects cosmic structure and archetypal patterns! Dreams, mythologies, television shows, music, societies, families...your life style mirrors cosmic patterns. The patterns are always the same. The time, circumstance and quality are different.

The more consciousness and light manifest in any person, event or thing the greater the quality, the more exactly it reflects cosmic patterns. The less consciousness and light manifest in any person, event or thing the more distorted are the cosmic patterns.

Begin viewing your life through the cosmological window. It will assist you in aligning your consciousness and energies with the cosmic process. Take a long, clear look at the male/female archetypal patterns in your life. How are your human relations with males: fathers, brothers, sons, husbands, etc.? With females: mothers, sisters, daughters, wives, etc.? Where are your relationships most active and least active?

If you're a male, what energies of the male archetype do you easily manifest? Manifest less easily? If you're a female, ask yourself the same questions.

When your relationships with a certain facet of the male or female archetype are harmonious the spiritual frequencies manifest with greater quality. When your relationship with a certain facet of the male or female archetype is inharmonious the spiritual frequencies manifest in a distorted way.

Pinpointing your inharmonious relationship patterns clearly indicates where you might choose to become more conscious and function more in harmony with the cosmic process.

From one point of view, your human relationship patterns in everyday life are a reflection of how you relate to different male/female aspects of yourself. Can you see how different aspects of yourself have male and female traits?

In this short section I've probably raised more questions than I've answered. Still, I wanted to introduce you to the view that cosmology is reflected in the pattern of your everyday life.

Asleep to the cosmic deep
Nothing to sow nor to reap;
Stirred by the divine spark,
The void splits light-dark.

Endless emanations of light,
Eternal day after eternal night;
The presence shapes forms,
The world's archetypal norms.

Experiences every dimension,
Every love and apprehension;
Now sowing, now reaping,
Living the last sleeping.

Light Wave 90

A Conscious Co-Creator

Once you become aware of how the archetypal patterns manifest in your life then you begin the process of becoming a conscious co-creator, a true, functional cosmocrat. Just think...the whole cosmos is continuously created, microsecond by microsecond, with polarity and shape as blueprints.

The more your microcosmos functions in accord with the macrocosmos the more you're the creator of your own life. As a conscious co-creator you become conscious of your structure. You get in touch with the facets of the human archetypes which are most in harmony with your purpose. And, as a result, you function accordingly; you do what most fulfills you.

What percentage of the earth's population do you think are conscious co-creators? At present, I would guess, less than 1%. That means 99% of the earth's population is out of sync, not in phase, unbalanced, inharmonious, unconscious, etc. No wonder there's so much war, poverty, famine, disease, hatred, greed, etc.

Signing peace treaties will not solve earth's problems. Feeding the starving will not solve earth's problems. Bettering the economic conditions will not solve earth's problems. Eradicating disease will not solve earth's problems.

These are all well and good. Unfortunately, they deal with effects not causes.

In the last section you read: "The more consciousness and light manifest in any person, event or thing the greater the quality, the more exactly it reflects cosmic patterns. The less consciousness and light manifest in any person, event or thing the more distorted are the cosmic patterns."

The cause of all our problems is unconsciousness, leading to distorted manifestation of cosmic patterns. In order to solve our problems each of us, one by one, must become more conscious. You must become more conscious of your cosmic connection, your cosmic heritage, the cosmic process.

One individual working day by day, month by month, year by year, lifetime by lifetime, to be more conscious and function more and more in accord with the cosmic process does more for his fellow earthling than all the do-gooders trying to feed the starving, eradicate disease, keep the peace, eliminate poverty, etc.

One conscious co-creator raises the vibration of every other person on the planet. Imagine what hundreds, thousands or even millions of conscious co-creators would do! The increased consciousness and light manifesting in the earth's people would decrease war, famine, poverty, disease, etc.

Societies, governments, institutions, corporations...individuals must give conscious co-creating the highest priority, the greatest value. Until that begins to happen the earth's problems will continue to multiply geometrically.

The way I see it right now there are just enough conscious co-creators and those becoming conscious co-creators to keep our collective head above water. The responsibility rests with the conscious ones. If we are to make the transition into the new age as a race on this planet, the conscious ones now on the planet must, first and foremost, continue to keep themselves aligned to the light and, second and foremost, they must assist through whatever means possible those beginning to become conscious.

Summary

1. Here the Science of Cosmology refers to all dimensions, worlds, levels of consciousness not just our four-dimensional space-time universe.
2. For the most part, traditional scientists do not acknowledge or even consider extrasensory perception a valid and accurate means of measuring/experiencing the cosmos.
3. Beyond the four-dimensional universe you enter the fifth dimension, the world of thought, feeling, emotion and desire... psychological forces, forms, fields and frequencies.
4. The study of cosmology goes beyond the fourth and fifth dimensions. Tuning to the Spiritual Frequencies begins in the sixth dimension, the world of light, love, wisdom, understanding, will...
5. Wherever you focus your attention and identify, that's where you are in the cosmos. The more conscious you are of where you're focusing your attention the more freedom and free will you have to contact and experience different levels of cosmic consciousness.
6. Tuning to the Spiritual Frequencies requires that you focus attention in the sixth and seventh dimensions.
7. You do not have to be an astronaut to explore the cosmos. You do not have to be a mystic, a yogi or a shaman to experience the multi-dimensional cosmos. If you can focus your attention steady for a time, your journey has begun. You have entered the *playground of the gods.*
8. Everything in the cosmos has a positive and negative polarity. Galaxies, solar systems, stars, planets...atoms, molecules, cells...people, places, things!
9. From the most mundane to the most sublime, polarity is the root structure of any unity.
10. As you experience cosmic structure more and more, I expect you will be changed forever. You will probably feel more integrated with the universe. Feelings of separateness will disappear or, at least, be reduced considerably.

11. There are archetypal patterns throughout the cosmos. The archetype is an original pattern or prototype.
12. All forms in the cosmos can be reduced to two geometric archetypes: 1) The circle and 2) The triangle.
13. Practice looking at things and people geometrically. Your experience of archetypal patterns will tune you into the cosmos.
14. All human archetypes can also be reduced to two: 1) Female and 2) Male.
15. The "as above" refers to the grand scheme of things and the "as below" refers to the human condition.
16. From another point of view there is no above or below. Once you establish and maintain your Tuning to the Spiritual Frequencies your perception changes. You begin to see-experience-feel that you live in one world, one multi-dimensional cosmos.
17. Whatever you look at reflects cosmic structure and archetypal patterns! The patterns are always the same; the time, circumstance and quality are different.
18. The more consciousness and light manifest in any person, event or thing the greater the quality, the more exactly it reflects cosmic patterns. The less consciousness and light manifest in any person, place or thing the more distorted are the cosmic patterns.
19. Once you become aware of how the archetypal patterns manifest in your life then you begin the process of becoming a conscious co-creator, a true, functional cosmocrat.
20. Just think...the whole cosmos is continuously created, microsecond by microsecond, with polarity and shape as blueprints.
21. The cause of all our problems is unconsciousness leading to distorted manifestation of cosmic patterns.
22. One individual working steadily to be more conscious, and function more and more in accord with the cosmic process does more for his fellow earthlings than all the do-gooders trying to feed the starving, eradicate disease, keep the peace, eliminate poverty, etc.

Chapter 19

The Science of Regeneration

Regeneration: Clearing The Path

Once you establish your connections to the spiritual frequencies, you will feel more in tune with yourself, others and the events in your life. In order to assist you in your spiritual quest it is wise to become aware of the regeneration process. Regeneration is the process of letting go habitual identifications.

Habitual identifications tend to automatically detune you from the spiritual frequencies. They energize pressure points of the past, leaving you in the grasp of compulsive behavior patterns.

Do you recall the last time you over-reacted emotionally, got upset, did something you regretted doing, etc.? The instant you automatically identified with the habitual pattern you went into a pressure point from a past experience. Identification with past patterns feeds them more energy; gives them continued life.

As an initiate on the path you must, sooner or later, come to terms with your pressure points of the past. You must clear your life path. You must consciously participate in the regeneration process.

Avoiding the regeneration process can be disasterous. Any teacher or teaching that does not include specific functional steps to eliminate habitual identifications will eventually be a deadend.

Your habits, compulsions, emotional reactions, obsessions are unbalanced anti-natural order vibrations. To assume you can continue on your path without letting go of destructive habits feeds the false personality, the negative part of the ego. Tapping higher energies, light frequencies, without eliminating destructive habits inflates the false personality.

Years ago I met a man who had not integrated the regeneration process into his spiritual work. Bill was a sincere, intense spiritual worker. His commitment to the inner life was enviable. Being in his presence made most people feel better, more centered, more alive.

Bill freely shared his knowledge with anyone who wished to listen and learn. One area of knowledge which was missing from his teachings was the regeneration skill. Bill was extremely intense. The higher force often made him overbearing to be around.

Bill was not consciously clearing his path: he was not eliminating pressure points of the past. Habits, compulsions, emotional reactions, obsessions are vibrations. With higher force, light, spiritual frequencies entering into Bill's auric-field, his pressure points were energized. Unbalanced behaviors manifested, disrupting his life and the life of others.

Several people attempted to communicate the critical importance of the regeneration process. He did not listen. He pushed blindly forward. The false personality became stronger. His body could not handle the mixture of old vibration and new light. He died unexpectedly of a heart attack at 38.

Now, this is an extreme example, but it dramatically emphasizes that avoiding the regeneration process can completely disrupt your spiritual quest. By squarely facing your past misdeeds and acknowledging honestly your daily unbalanced behaviors you take a giant step into the regenerative process.

Once you've taken the all important first step, continue monitoring your behaviors. Acknowledge habits and begin a long-term effort to eventually stop automatically identifying with them.

Many negative behavior patterns will fall away simply by being more conscious. Other pressure points will relentlessly persist. You must persist as well. In the next section, I will offer you a number of functional methods to help you eliminate particularly stubborn habits.

The cosmic flame
Has no name;
Silence is its voice,
Feelings of rejoice.

Touch the peace-power,
Feel the forces flower;
Ripples of life
Cast out strife.

Hold your attention,
Quiet the mention;
Feel its force,
Here is the source.

Light Wave 91

Regeneration: An Octave Function

In Chapter 8 I told you about octave functions. An octave function is several ways (at least 7 or 8) of working on one thing.

In order to cultivate your regenerative skills here are eight functions.

Subconscious
1. Digesting past experiences
2. Write it out
3. Touch and let go

Superconscious
4. E-therapy
5. Asking forgiveness
6. Invocation

Conscious
7. Non-identification
8. Offering meditation

Each function regenerates from either a subconscious, superconscious or conscious level as indicated. I will give you a brief "how to" of each function. Try them; test them; see what happens.

#1 Digesting Past Experiences

In our fast-paced technological world, we experience at an accelerated rate. By the time we're 20-25 we have experienced as much as two or three lifetime's compared to a person living a hundred or two hundred years ago.

We need to take time to digest past experiences. And how do you do that? You simply take time to sit quietly and review in your mind's eye what you've done, who you've interacted with and where you've been.

There's no need to analyze, judge or criticize. Just look and see. Just observe. Notice patterns. Ten or fifteen minutes at a time is plenty.

#2 Write It Out

Do you harbor any antagonisms, hatreds, grudges, resentments, anger, hostility, etc? To regenerate, to feel better, you need to discharge that pent-up energy.

Choose an overpowering emotion that you're struggling with, get a pad of paper and a pen and write it out. Get emotional. Write intensely, wildly. Anything and everything about the emotion - write it. Please do not write neatly. Forget that. Scribble if you have to, but write emotionally.

After ten, fifteen, twenty minutes, stop. Please, do not read what you've written. Rip it up into little pieces and throw it in the garbage.

#3 Touch And Let Go

If you have any particular subconscious blocks with any situation, person or life area, write it down describing what it is in a few words. Place the piece of paper on a table and sit down. Now, hold your hands palms down just over the piece of paper.

Next, touch what you've written on the paper with both hands (with the upper half of the fingers). Then, let go. Repeat. Touch and let go! Keep it up for 5-10-15 minutes. Use your judgement. If you're tired or feel you've done enough stop after five minutes. Ten or fifteen minutes is more than enough especially in the beginning.

When you're done, rip the paper up and throw it away. Be sure to rest, listen to music, read a book, etc., for at least a half hour to an hour afterwards. It is wise to set aside quiet time after any of the regenerative exercises.

#4 E-therapy

I was fortunate to come across this regenerative method years ago. Sit comfortably. Next, say to yourself out loud:

> *"I ask my mind (Higher Self, Superconscious)*
> *To take whatever steps are necessary*
> *To remove whatever is blocking it."*

Repeat this phrase at rhythmic intervals for five or ten minutes.

#5 Asking Forgiveness

If you have ever taken a good look at your past deeds I'm sure many were not exactly acceptable. Face it; we have all done our share of ill deeds. Whether in this life or another, we have done some things we regreted.

Asking forgiveness using the following affirmation (write your own if you prefer) will eliminate the guilts and attachments to past offenses.

> *"Infinite divine presence I ask forgiveness for all offenses against the natural order in this lifetime and all other lifetimes. I ask forgiveness not only for myself but for all my relatives and ancestors in this lifetime and all others. I ask forgiveness for all errors in thought, word and action. Release me from all attachments to negative memories. Transmute the negative energies into the limitless ever-present light of love and wisdom. Let it be. So be it. Aumen"*

Say this affirmation, preferably out loud, three times. Say it with all the genuine sincerity you can muster. The divine presence will respond.

#6 Invocation

An invocation is a request for divine intervention. You ask a higher power, a more-evolved being, to give you a helping hand. God knows we can all use it. Here's an example. Go ahead and use it if you like. Write your own invocation to suit your own preference.

> *"Oh Christos, Cosmic Being, by your grace, love and divine compassion I ask you to transform, transmute and transfigure the base metals of sense, desire, emotion and mood into the crystal clear light of Christ consciousness. Vibrate the force of your Christ frequencies into the psychic field and dissolve and destroy the negative vibrations which interfere with the immediate manifestations of the cosmic Christos consciousness through love, compassion, grace and wisdom. Let it be. So be it. Aumen"*

Say the invocation out loud with a strong voice and a deeply sincere heart. At the conclusion of each reading clap once, *clap*; clap twice, *clap, clap*; clap three times, *clap, clap, clap*.

If possible spend a quiet half hour to an hour after the invocation. Read some quality information; listen to some uplifting music, etc.

#7 Non-identification

As you go about your day stop identifying with every little upset, annoyance, negative thought, dislike, etc. Be more conscious. Observe your reactions.

Non-identification is an effective regeneration tool. Notice your intense reactions. Pause... you have a choice. You can make a choice whether or not you'll go along with that thought, emotion, word or action.

#8 Offering Meditation

Take a meditation posture that you find comfortable. Now visualize all your energies flowing upward toward the top of your head, the crown center. Keep it up. All energies, all vibrations of thought, image, emotion, feeling, desire, etc. are flowing toward the force center at the top of the head.

At the same time all your forces are flowing to the crown, genuinely, sincerely, deeply offer all your energies to the one presence, the one power, the one process, the one plan. This regeneration method hinges on the offering. You must be willing to give it all, offer it all. The regeneration will follow as day follows night.

> *Contact the Christ-field,*
> *God-energies revealed;*
> *Thought-emotion still,*
> *Light forces fill.*
>
> *Hold attention at the crown,*
> *Halts the psychic frown;*
> *Quiet the mental chatter,*
> *Feel light in matter.*
>
> *Meditate as you do,*
> *The life force will renew;*
> *Pay attention to the light,*
> *Receive the blessed rite.*
>
> *Light Wave 92*

Family Patterns

Before you can enter fully into the regeneration process you must become conscious of what requires regeneration. The family force-field is an excellent place to start.

Every family has its particular family patterns. There are common:
- Thought Patterns
- Speech Patterns
- Emotional Patterns
- Physical Patterns
- Desire Patterns
- Goal Patterns
- Feeling Patterns
- Etc.

It doesn't take much effort to see every family has its patterns. Are you aware of your family patterns? Tuning to the Spiritual Frequencies requires awareness of family patterns both constructive and destructive.

Those family patterns that are in harmony with your nature, with your structure and function, you want to utilize. Those family patterns that are inharmonious with your nature, with your structure and function, you want to eliminate.

How are family patterns formed in you? The family is a force-field. The forces in the field include thought, feeling, belief, action, speech, desire, etc., vibrations. The vibrations in the family force-field are built up over hundreds, even thousands of years. The constructive and destructive vibration patterns are usually very powerful and are easily transferred from one family member to another by emanation and absorbtion.

While in your mother's womb, family patterns begin to take form. Thoughts, attitudes, feelings, emotions, voice tones are sensed by the evolving baby. Once the baby is born its highly sensitive sympathetic nervous system absorbs mother's vibrations at an incredible rate. At a less accelerated rate, baby absorbs other family members' vibrations.

The emanation and absorbtion process usually goes on for at least twenty years. No wonder family behavior patterns are so deeply ingrained in the subconscious.

Now, if a family member feels an inner urge to develop their individuality, often the family patterns will assert a powerful force of resistance. Individuality means changes, variations and perhaps even the elimination of family patterns.

The family force-field strongly resists major changes. If you want to develop your spiritual path, then the family will be less important. You will give greater value to your spiritual source than your worldly source. As a result, the family force-field and patterns get less energy.

Many family patterns can be extremely destructive to an individual awakening to spiritual frequencies. Dogmatic religious beliefs, for example, can stunt spiritual evolution. A tremendous inner tension and conflict can war within, one pulled between traditional beliefs and present inner experiences.

When you discover a family pattern that is undermining your evolution into individuality and spirituality you must apply the regenerative process. Utilize some of the regeneration skills outlined in the previous section. You must reduce the pull of negative family patterns in order to stabilize in the spiritual frequencies.

Be persistent. Do not underestimate the power of negative family patterns. They will not leave you just because you wish them away. The force of your new individual patterns must have more force than the family pattern force. It's simply a question of psychological physics.

Observe what happens to you when you're around your family. Do you feel more centered or less centered? Are you more energetic or less energetic? Are you more aware or less aware? Observe yourself, observe your family members. Become conscious of family patterns.

Caught in action's craze,
Blind in a life maze;
Running, rushing, doing,
No time for rest-reviewing.

Stop the mad greed dance,
Give yourself a chance;
Make time for light-tune,
Feel the spiritual boon.

Alternate action-rest,
That seems to be the best;
Keeps you stable and strong,
Your cells singing a song.

Light Wave 93

Frequencies Of The Race Psyches

First of all, what do I mean by race psyche? Most can tell the difference between an Englishman and a Frenchman, between a German and a Russian and so on. Different belief systems, thought patterns, codes, laws, taboos, customs, cultural inclinations, etc. come together to manifest different race psyches.

The energy vibrations of thought, feeling, emotion, desire, belief, attitude, action, etc. are the frequencies of a race psyche or F-O-R-Ps for short. Whatever culture, society or country you're born into has specific F-O-R-Ps that are peculiar to its psyche. A Russian behaves very differently from an American. An Aborigine behaves very differently from an Australian.

The way you think, act, feel, emote, desire, react, relate...has a lot to do with the frequencies of your race psyche. The regeneration process requires that you be conscious of all influences. Remember, whatever you're unconscious of controls you. The spiritual frequencies, then, cannot manifest in a completely balanced way.

Certain FORPs, for example, can turn you away from the light. Let's say financial and materialistic FORPs grasp your attention to the point of excess. You may very well accumulate great wealth, but what are the consequences to your natural structure/function?

Identification with some FORPs for some people can lead to self-destruction.

Visualize a building in the Los Angeles area. One day a mild earthquake, 3.5 on the Richter scale, shakes the building slightly. There's no damage. At another time, a more powerful earthquake strikes, 6.7 on the Richter scale. This time a few windows break, pictures crash off walls, and light fixtures shatter.

When the great earthquake hits, 8.5 on the Richter scale, the foundation shifts, walls crack, steel beams snap, the building crumbles. The forces acting on the building's structure have exceeded its NTP, normal temperature and pressure. It's purely a matter of physics.

Some FORPs act much like earthquakes do on a building. That's why it's critical for one to Tune to the Spiritual Frequencies. Be conscious of FORPs. Any FORP that you unconsciously and automatically identify with is a potential earthquake force to your psychological structure.

In January 1986, the Challenger astronauts died in a fiery explosion. Within minutes most Americans felt the emotional impact of the tragic accident. The mass media accelerated the emotional reaction through the American race psyche and then through the race psyches of the world. Do you see how powerful a FORP can be?

What FORPs do you unconsciously identify with? Here are a few you might consider:

- The work ethic
- Judeo-Christian belief systems
- Democratic principles
- Free enterprise economics
- Government-sponsored education
- Marriage
- Sexual mores
- English language identification
- Dietary patterns
- Scientific principles
- Etc.

Of course, if you like, you can take each area listed and break it down into its component FORPs.

Once you discover a FORP that consistently detunes you from the spiritual frequencies, it is time to detune yourself from the FORP. Use the regeneration octave function. It will assist you with the detachment process.

Observe your thought-feel-mood,
Psychic energies brewed;
The outer starts from the inner,
Ignorance makes a sinner.

Thought-action-event,
That's how life is spent;
Choose carefully your thought,
Or in chaos-actions caught.

Learn the cosmic laws,
Apply it to your flaws;
Transform your suffering soul,
Into a light being whole

Light Wave 94

Past Life Patterns

On a recent trip to Minneapolis I did a Pendulum Life Reading for a psychologist. (See *Beyond Pendulum Power* by Greg Nielsen). She wanted to know if I could pinpoint why she was so anxious about raising her hourly fee. She raised her rates from $25 an hour to $30 an hour.

This modest increase unleashed a whole range of emotions. She was afraid she might be overcharging, despite the fact that the average hourly fee in Minneapolis was $40-50 an hour at that time. She was afraid her regular patients could not afford the additional $5 a visit.

Suddenly her patient load began to drop. She, then, felt she had made a really big mistake. She was afraid her practice would crumble.

She realized the emotional knot she had tied herself in. She wanted to untie herself from her unrealistic and self-destructive fear.

Before becoming a psychologist she was a nun. Intuitively, she felt her vow of poverty contributed to her fear. I asked the pendulum on a 0-10 scale how strong an influence does Joan's previous vow of poverty have on her present money anxieties? The answer was a ten!

Joan responded in amazement, "I haven't been a nun for twenty years, how could the vow of poverty still have such a powerful hold on my subconscious"?

At that point, I brought up the possibility that she might have had several lives in convents. She agreed that it might make sense. It would certainly explain the gripping power of her anxiety.

I used the pendulum to tune into her past lives. I specifically wanted to pinpoint the lifetime where the vow of poverty received its most powerful hold.

I asked,"When was the lifetime that the vow of poverty asserted its present strength"? I asked, "50 years, 100 years...450 years"? At 450 years the pendulum answered yes.

I continued asking questions until we found out that around 1536 she was a monk living in a monestery in France. The head abbot was a fire and brimstone kind of guy who pounded his monks with the fear of god. Joan, in that lifetime as a monk, became so afraid of breaking the vow of poverty that she believed she would burn in hell for eternity if she even thought of better living conditions.

Being aware of this past life pattern Joan was able to let out a sigh of relief. She knew now where it all began. The money anxiety already had less of a grip on her subconscious.

I suggested she go to a library and check out a book that focused on the monastic life in France in the 16th century. Then I told her to do "touch and let goes" on the book. Simply touch the book with both hands and let go for ten or fifteen minutes once a week for a few weeks.

If you have a stubborn habit or compulsion that you've tried to break or overcome with little or no success, it may be a past life pattern. By tracking down the lifetime that has the greatest negative force, you begin to neutralize its hold on you. You can continue neutralizing its power by utilizing the regenerative methods given earlier in this chapter.

Naturally, not everybody has the knack of tracking down past life patterns. Use your intuition. Ask yourself, "Where in history does my present problem have a traditional counterpart"? Take note of your present interests and inclinations. When and where in history were they prominent cultural forces.

The poverty mentality, for example, was a major cultural force in medieval Christianity.

Bathe in fiery force,
Feel the mighty source;
Transmutes the rigid hold
Of fixed moods frozen cold.

Steady your attention,
Focus without tension;
Turn it toward the light,
Awakens inner sight.

The body-psyche shell
Think it's you, that's your hell;
Let go of attachment,
Enter light's detachment.

Light Wave 95

The Alchemical Transmutation

In 1970 and '71 I had the good fortune of having a lot of free time to study, research, contemplate and meditate. One strong study focus at that time was alchemy. Alchemy is the ancient and medieval science of transforming base metals into gold.

Please...true alchemy was not taken literally. A true alchemist did not believe he could transmute lead into gold. Rather, he was intent on transmuting the base vibrations of mood, desire, emotion and sense into the spiritual vibrations of love, light and wisdom.

The science of regeneration is the specific process by which you can transmute a lower degenerate vibration into a higher regenerate vibration. As you become more and more conscious of the exact instant that you feel, identify and register a negative vibration, a mysterious and miraculous opportunity arises. In an instantaneous act of will and awareness you can see-feel the negative vibration as light. Presto! Magic! You transmute base energy into light....literally!

During that 1970-71 cycle of rich, rewarding and fruitful study, I devoted a lot of time to learning all I could about "the light". I discovered the light is a high vibration energy, a frequency beyond the range of everyday sensory awareness. Yet, as I began to see, we are surrounded by light.

I began to see, touch, feel everything is light, everyone is light, every place is light, every thought is light, every emotion is light, every desire is light. I practiced this exercise from the time I got up until the time I went to sleep. Often, I even kept it up in my dreams.

Gradually, I became more and more interested in the alchemical transmutation process. It eventually dawned on me that I might be able to see-feel a negative vibration as light.

One day, after a particularly avid study session, I left my apartment and boarded a bus. I resolved that no matter what I felt or saw riding the bus I would see-feel it as light.

I sat down. I glanced at the other passengers. I was observing myself as light, every other passenger as light and everything on the bus as light.

At one point my eyes briefly stopped and peered into the eyes of a female passenger in her mid-thirties. She must have been in a bad mood because a wave of hostility emanated from her toward me. As my eyes left hers and continued scanning, the hostility reached me. We're talking a second for all of this to transpire.

Remember, I was seeing-feeling everything as light. Even the wave of hostility I saw-felt as light. Something momentous happened. As the hostility reached and entered my aura I saw-felt its light and it became light. I felt a sudden surge of increased life force.

"My god", I said to myself, "this is alchemy. This is the transmutation of base metals into gold." Even as I write this, recalling my discovery many years ago, tingling sensations are vibrating up and down my spine.

The negative hostile energy suddenly became energizing light. Since that day, I have experienced the transmutation of lead into gold...the water of emotion into the wine of spiritual regeneration.

One of the functions of present-now consciousness is to choose to see-feel negative, vitality-lowering energies as light and then experience the energizing effects of transmutation. This conscious transmutating skill is available to you. Please try it. Practice. Keep practicing until you get it.

When you begin transmutating base vibration into spiritual golden light you will be a regenerator. You will not be drained by negative energies. As the alchemists said and wrote repeatedly, "the gold is in the dung".

Summary

1. Regeneration is the process of letting go habitual identifications. Habitual identifications detune you from the spiritual frequencies. They energize pressure points of the past, leaving you in the grasp of compulsive behavior patterns.
2. As an initiate on the path, you must sooner or later come to terms with your pressure points of the past. You must clear your life path. You must consciously participate in the regeneration process.
3. Tapping higher energies, light frequencies, without eliminating destructive habits inflates the false personality.
4. By squarely facing your past misdeeds and acknowledging honestly your daily unbalanced behaviors you take a giant step into the regeneration process.
5. Regeneration: an octave function...subconscious: 1) digesting past experiences, 2) write it out and 3) touch and let go...superconscious: 4) E-therapy, 5) asking forgiveness and 6) invocation...conscious: 7) non-identification and 8) offering meditation.
6. Are you aware of your family patterns? Tuning to the Spiritual Frequencies requires awareness of family patterns both constructive and destructive.
7. Those family patterns that are in harmony with your nature, with your structure and function, you want to utilize. Those family patterns that are inharmonious with your nature, with your structure and function, you want to eliminate.
8. The vibrations in the family force-field are built up over hundreds, even thousands of years. The constructive and destructive vibration patterns are usually very powerful and are easily transfered from one family member to another by emanation and absorbtion.
9. The emanation and absorbtion process casually goes on for at least twenty years. No wonder family behavior patterns are so deeply ingrained in the subconscious.

10. Many family patterns can be extremely destructive to an individual awakening to spiritual frequencies. Dogmatic religious beliefs, for example, can stunt spiritual evolution.
11. Be persistent. Do not underestimate the power of negative family patterns. They will not leave you just because you wish them away. The force of your new individual patterns must have more force than the family pattern force. It's simply a question of psychological physics.
12. Different belief systems, thought patterns, codes, laws, taboos, customs, cultural inclinations, etc. come together to manifest different race psyches.
13. The energy vibrations of thought, feeling, emotion, desire, belief, attitude, action, etc. are the frequencies of a race psyche, or F-O-R-Ps for short.
14. Identification with some FORPs for some people can lead to self-destruction.
15. Once you discover a FORP that consistently detunes you from the spiritual frequencies it is time to detune yourself from the FORP.
16. If you have a stubborn habit or compulsion that you've tried to break or overcome with little or no success, it may be a past-life pattern.
17. By tracking down the lifetime that has the greatest negative force you begin to neutralize a habit's hold on you.
18. A true alchemist did not believe he could transmute lead into gold. Rather, he was intent on transmuting the base vibrations of mood, desire, emotion and sense into the spiritual vibrations of love, light and wisdom.
19. The Science of Regeneration is the specific process by which you can transmute a lower degenerate vibration into a higher regenerate vibration.
20. In an instantaneous act of awareness and will you can see-feel the negative vibration as light. Presto! Magic! You transmute base energy into light...literally!

Chapter 20

Becoming a Light Being

The Empyrean

"And this I know: whether the one True Light
Kindle to Love, or Wrath consume me quite,
One glimpse of It within the tavern caught
Better than in the temple lost outright."

From Rubaiyat of Omar Khayyam

I am home in the Light. All around, ubiquitous golden, diamond Light. I am living breathing Light. I am conscious Light without form.

A memory of a body is dim. I feel a minute change in the circulation of Light, the pull of gravity. I have returned to Light. I feel myself again.

I have no eyes yet I see Light. I have no ears yet I hear Light. I have no hands yet I touch Light. I have no tongue yet I taste Light. I have no nose yet I smell Light.

All senses blend into one supersense. I feel whole, one, united. I have never felt anything else.

Time is meaningless. Timelessness is all there is. Beyond time there is no time. Timelessness is all there is, therefore, there is no concept of timelessness.

Love permeates my Light presence. I am moved by Divine Will to emanate the Light. I radiate Light directing It to all who require more Light.

Wisdom circulates in my vortex of Light. Wisdom measures the Light...one infinity, two infinity, three infinity...infinite infinity. The smallest speck of Light is all Light.

I am a Light Being again. I sigh. My consciousness expands several infinities.

I have traveled through gravity realms. I know the electro-magnetic spectrum. I have lived in the atomic nuclei.

The Empyrean is my home, the source of sources. God Consciousness is all I know. I am detached from all else.

I function the way God functions. I am God, a part of God. I know nothing else. I have no concept of It.

The Light regenerates. Consciousness is rejuvenated. The Light has made me strong again. Divine Will moves me. I have but one task: Circulate the Light.

The thought of my task attracts a body. I am strong in the Light now. A body does not feel so heavy. It is only a tool by which I can Circulate the Light to those who have forgotten the Light.

I attract those who long once again for the Light. They are hungry. I feed them Light. They are nourished; I am nourished.

Those who need the Light absorb the Light. They are regenerated and rejuvenated. I long for the Light. I leave my body.

I soar through space-time. Planets, stars, galaxies, super-galaxies are flickers of consciousness. Beyond the speed of Light I enter the realm of Light, Empyrean, pure Light.

I am home once again, the Limitless Light. It is cool Light. It transmutes: memories of form, memories of gravity, memories of pain, memories of suffering, memories of disease, memories of death.

I am a Light Being in a Dynamic Light World. I breath the Forever Concealed Divine Presence. My thoughts are Archetypes. My Will is Creation. I hear only the AUM.

My brothers are Light Beings. My sisters are Light Beings. My father is God. My mother is Goddess.

Polarity is the eternal battery of my being, generating Light forever. I is Light. Am is consciousness of Light. Being is Light functioning as Light.

I am a Light Being in a Dynamic Light World. The Empyrean, Sat San...True Home, The Realm of Light...I never left, I never returned...I leave and I return.

Place your attention on the Light my friend. Gently hold your attention steadily on the Light...The nectar of the gods, manna from heaven, the aqua divinum...You are a Light Being in a Dynamic Light World...the Empyrean Here-Now.

Light In The Body

> *"Every man has a little spark of the sun*
> *in his own bosom...a spark of the original*
> *light is suppose to remain deep down in the*
> *interior of every atom."*

> *Hargrave Jennings*
> *Rosicrucian, 1872*

In November of 1932, Dr. George W. Crile of the Cleveland Laboratories announced a remarkable discovery. Deep in the heart of every plant, animal and human cell he discovered a foci of energy with estimated temperatures of from 3,000 to 6,000 degress F. He called these tiny suns "hot points" or "radiogens".

Dr. Crile wrote of his research, "who would think that there are hot points in man and animals on the order of the temperature of the surface of the sun? If one could look into protoplasm with an eye capable of infinite magnification, one might expect to see radiogens spaced like stars, as suns in infinite miniature.

Without exaggeration the concept may be taken to mean that within the very flesh of man burns the fierce fire of the sun, and that within man's body glow infinitely small counterparts of the stars!"

As human beings we are structured to function mentally, emotionally, physically, consciously, creatively, etc. We have the capability of registering, experiencing and harnessing a vast range of vibrations, frequencies and energies on physiological and psychological levels.

As human beings we are also structured to function spiritually. We can align ourselves with light frequencies. You are a Light Being in a Dynamic Light World.

Physically you are composed of trillions of cells. Everyone of your cells has a star glowing in its center. Our Milky Way Galaxy!

No doubt about it, we are Light Beings. You can know it intellectually. You can even get emotionally excited. Still, how do you experience the Light? How can you Tune into the Spiritual Frequencies?

Many of us have been ignorant and unconscious of our spiritual heritage, the Light. We learn nothing about it in school, at home, from church. Most of the learning emphasis in our race psyche is placed on the physical, emotional and mental levels.

A few of us also learn how to be creative. Even fewer learn how to be conscious. Every once in a while one will tune into the Light and rediscover their spiritual heritage.

If you feel drawn to the Light, there are some specific, definite, simple steps you can take. Remember, your conditioning for many years has been mostly physical, emotional and mental. The resistance of your past conditioning must be overcome by the force of your personal effort.

Say to yourself, or out loud if you prefer:

My feet are Light
My calves are Light
My knees are Light
My thighs are Light
My sex center is Light
My hips are Light
My back side is Light
My stomach is Light
My chest is Light
My hands are Light
My arms are Light
My shoulders are Light
My spine and back are Light
My neck and throat are Light
My chin is Light
My face is Light
My eyes are Light
My ears are Light
My mouth is Light
My insides are Light
My aura is Light
I am Light
I am a Light Being in a Dynamic Light World
Feel-know each part, all of you is Light.

Repeat this exercise as often as it feels comfortable.

Be sure to feel-know each part, all of you is Light. Bring your attention to each part as you say it.

Here is another exercise. Whatever you touch, whatever you see...whoever you touch...whoever you see, say to yourself, "this is Light".

The pen I'm writing with is Light, the desk is Light, the person walking into my office is Light...etc. Keep it up all day long.

The Light is mystical. The Light is practical. You do not have to wait until physical death to experience the Light. You can experience it today, right now!

Place your attention on the Light my friend. Gently hold your attention steadily on the Light. You are a Light Being in a dynamic Light World.

Each must find his way,
Step by step each day
Discover your structure,
Delusions puncture.

When on your true path,
You feel bliss' warm bath;
A path with a heart
Never tears you apart.

See what you must do,
Your actions will renew;
Every cell aglow,
Life energies flow.

Light Wave 96

Seven Steps To Light

"The Gnostics believed that human beings,
carry within them from the beginning a
higher element deriving from the World
of Light, which enables them to rise
above the World of the Seven into the
Upper World of Light."

Carl Jung

There are seven prerequisites that must be mastered before the Light can shine in your life continuously.
1. A functionally trained mind
2. Purification of the psychic centers
3. Emotional control and calm
4. Physical repose
5. Measured speech
6. Creative use of energy
7. Living with purpose
Let's give a rough description of each of these seven.

ONE   A functionally trained mind can analyze, synthesize, consciously abstract, concentrate, visualize and go into neutral. A trained mind is flexible, steady, widely read, intelligently curious, penetrating, measuring and discriminative.

It knows the difference between fantasy and fact. It is not afraid of long, hard thinking. It is not afraid of not knowing. It is both receptive and active to the outer and the inner.

TWO Purification of the psychic centers. Locked in the cells of your body are the frozen energies and memories of past traumatic happenings. These difficult experiences must be resolved by employing various techniques of elimination.

These negative vibrations of matter must be excreted before the Light can enter and stay. As the saying goes, you cannot put new wine into old bottles.

You cannot put the higher Light into a body and psyche full of negative forces like dark thoughts, black emotions, crimson desires and lust-red passions. The Light would only fatten the swine and lower you into a black pit of doom.

THREE Emotional control and calm. Habitual automatic reactions to words, images, ideas, events, etc. set in motion chain reactions of negative emotional energies. Gradually, you must train yourself to register but not react to any emotional frequency. This demands long and determined observation of your emotional center.

You must thoroughly learn what your emotional reaction patterns are. Next, you will detach from them by reacting less and less to any emotional pattern.

FOUR Physical repose. How can the Light circulate in a body that is rigid, tense and inflexible? It's impossible.

Tension in the body and tuning to the Light are incompatible. Once, however, you resolve to let the tensions go to some degree, tuning to the Light will assist the relaxation process. The art of relaxation is a must if you are to fully enjoy the Light Frequencies.

A tense body reflects an attitude of extreme identification with things. Physical repose practiced throughout the day opens a channel to the Light.

FIVE Measured speech. Vibrating to the Light manifests more power. If you were to be unmeasured in your speech, yet full of Light, your words could set destructive influences into motion.

By rigorous training in the Science of General Semantics, you use words as signs and symbols which are clear and accurate. Measured speech transmutes dark confusion into light clarity.

SIX Creative use of energy. This means you expend your energies wisely in procreation and sexual recreation. Excess leads to unbalance. Too much unbalance reduces the degree of Light.

Finding your own natural rhythm of sexual satisfaction which combines communication, affection and physical pleasures seems to be the way to go. Sublimation of energy into creative outlets is highly recommended. It is an excellent preparation for creation of lighted forms.

SEVEN Living with purpose. As you get to know yourself better, you begin to experience a kind of "inner glow", an influx of high energy when you do certain things. The "inner glow" is a signal telling you that a certain activity is part of your life purpose.

Become sensitive to how you feel when you do certain tasks. The rush of high energy is a manifestation of Light. When you live with purpose you radiate Light continuously.

If you are not living with purpose, resolve to find it. Accept the quest. Explore, search, test, experience. You will find it. If you have found your purpose be grateful and pursue it diligently.

> *Return the forces to light;*
> *The elements will fight,*
> *Stubbornly resist the flow*
> *And feel the cosmic glow.*
>
> *Detach from impulse action,*
> *Automatic reaction*
> *And thought-image delusion;*
> *Return to light world fusion.*
>
> *Lift the forces to the field,*
> *The Apocalypse unsealed;*
> *Centered in the master light*
> *Awakens spiritual sight.*
>
> *Light Wave 97*

Light Around The Body

> *"One is able to see a beautific glow*
> *radiating above and around all objects*
> *and things. It appears like a shimmering*
> *silvery aura and turns the mundane*
> *world into a fairyland."*
>
> *Vitvan*

Getting up in the morning can be a struggle, a fight, a battle for one who desires self-unfoldment from unconscious identification with matter (things, words, materialism). Going through the day can be even more difficult. People's auras are polluted with foul decay of black thought, flame desire, heat emotion, etc.

Maintaining a conscious center in the midst of this chaos borders on the impossible. The negative energies emanating and vibrating from people and places, auras and atmospheres builds up destructive force-fields. When you find your energy level dropping, it may be time to consciously connect with the Light.

The Light will protect and regenerate you, repulsing the negative emanations of destructive thought, feeling, desire, emotion, etc. At the same time whatever psychic pollutants have collected in your aura will be transmuted by the Light into finer frequencies and wavelengths of energy.

Your strength, focus and tuning will return so that you can survive the turbulent psychic waves almost constantly vibrating through the race psyche force-field.

Naturally, in order to visualize the Light while on the job or in social situations, you must be able to concentrate. Your mind has to be steady, yet flexible.

Steady because you have to focus continually on the Light, and flexible because you have to continue with whatever activity is at hand with awareness.

There are several ways of visualizing the Light surrounding and interpenetrating your aura. I will present two ways.

Visualization #1: Visualize a radiant egg of White Light. See figure #16 on page 208. Visualize yourself in the midst, in the center of this spiraling, pulsating force-field of Light.

See yourself bathing in the spiraling, spinning force-field of White Light. See the coils turning in a clockwise direction. See the spirals turning in and out.

Feel the Light transmuting the tensions into repose. Sense the Light melting fixed icy thoughts and subconscious attitudes. Let go of rigid identification with your body. Transfer identification to the force-field of Light.

The coiling force-field of White Light transforms your aura into an electromagnet, giving you a certain degree of strength.

Three factors determine the strength of an electromagnet:

1. The number of turns. An increase of turns in a coil increases the magnetic strength of the coil.
2. The amount of current. (The intensity of your visualization.) If you increase the amount of current in a coil, the magnetic strength increases.
3. Permeability of the core. (The core in this case is your physical, etheric, astral and mental bodies.) The core of the coil is the material within the coil. Permeability is the ability of a substance to conduct magnetic lines of force easily.

The spinning electromagnetic force-field of Light has a transmuting, purifying effect.

Recording studios, radio and TV stations, have what they call a bulker. It is a large electromagnet which is passed over a tape in order to erase any sound previously recorded. In this way the tape is cleaned, cleared, ready to be used again.

You can, in effect, bulk your aura. By visualizing the Light. The Light erases some of the recordings on your body, subconscious mind and conscious mind. Once your aura is cleansed, you see more clearly.

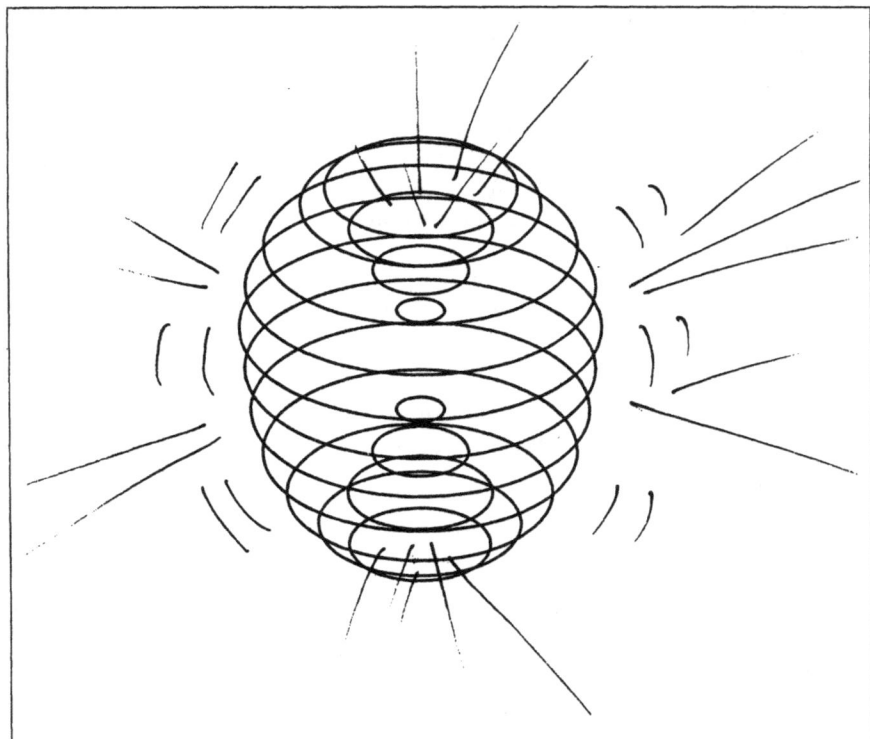

Figure 16: Egg of Light

A beam of light descends,
Sent by light being friends;
Transmutes the psychic mire
Into the star-field fire.

The light is no timid force,
It has no time for remorse;
It churns and burns the past,
Into the lake of fire cast.

The light has healing power,
A cleansing aura shower;
Give thanks to the god-light
Transforms the meek to might.

Light Wave 98

Invoking The Light

> *"And he was transfigured before them;*
> *and his face did shine as the sun, and*
> *his garments became white as the Light."*
>
> Matthew 17:2

By invoking the Light you attract the Light to you. The invoking process is simply an asking with deep sincerity, gratitude and reverence that the frequencies of Light protect, assist, purify and enlighten.

Invoking the Light can be beneficial any time. There are, however, times when the Light can be especially helpful.

Before going to sleep at night it is wise to invoke the Light. The day's vibrations linger in the aura. These include thoughts, feelings, emotions, events, actions, attitudes, desires, etc. The lingering vibrations or stale magnetism must be released or transmuted for regenerative restful sleep.

Use the following invocation of Light or write your own. You can speak aloud or read silently whichever you prefer.

An Invocation of the Light:

> *Oh Cosmic Light, radiant, vibrant and*
> *brilliant, regenerate, transform and*
> *transmute the base substance of sense,*
> *desire and emotion into the luminous*
> *wavelength of balanced Christos Light.*
> *May every cell bathe in Light; may*
> *every thought bathe in Light; may*
> *My consciousness bathe in Light.*
> *Aumen.*

Invoke the Light before meditation and prayer. The Light, the Spiritual Frequencies you feel, will set the tone of your meditation or prayer. Your spiritual communion will be felt more definitely and deeply. Its effects will stay with you longer.

Invoke the Light when you awake in the morning. Dream images and sleepiness often keep us in a semi-conscious state first thing in the morning. By invoking the Light you focus your awareness squarely in the here-now.

Invoke the Light in times of trouble. When major and minor crises strike remember the Light, invoke the Light. Chaotic thoughts, emotions and actions are ordered by Light.

"Then I saw that on the shaft there hung
a human figure that held within itself
all the loneliness of the world and of the
spaces. Alone, and hoping for nothing, the
one hung and gazed down into the void. For
long the one gazed, drawing all solitude unto
itself. Then deep in the fathomless dark was
born an infinitesmal spark. Slowly, it rose
from the bottomless depth, and as it rose it
grew until it became a star. And the star
hung in space just opposite the figure, and
the White Light streamed upon the lonely one."

From The Inner Word of Man *by Frances Wickes*

I'd like to say something about the word "Christos" in the invocations. It does not refer to Jesus the man or Jesus the Christ, the so-called son of God. Christos was a term used in the ancient Greek mystery schools to describe an initiate who remembered and reclaimed his divine status as a Light Being.

Invocation

Oh Christos, cosmic being...by
your grace, love and divine
compassion, I ask you to transform,
transmute and transfigure the
base metals of sense, desire, emotion
and mood into the crystal clear
light of Christ consciousness.
Vibrate the force of your Christ
frequencies into the psychic
field and dissolve and destroy
the negative vibrations which
interfere with the immediate
manifestation of the cosmic Christos
consciousness through love, compassion,
grace and wisdom.

Let it be, so be it.
Aumen

The Body of Light

> *"The esotericist understands that true
> self-knowledge can be attained only
> through self-development in the highest
> possible sense of the term, a develop-
> ment which begins with introspection
> and the awakening of creative and re-
> generative forces which now slumber in
> man's inner protoplasmic nature, like
> the vivific potency in the ovum, and
> which when roused into activity trans-
> forms him ultimately into a divine
> being bodied in a deathless ethereal
> form of ineffable beauty."*
>
> James M. Pryse, The Apocalypse Unsealed

Everyone acknowledges the existence of their physical body. You can touch it. You can move it. You feed it. You wash it, etc.

Besides the physical body there's an energy body. Not everyone acknowledges the existence of the energy body. The energy body interpenetrates the physical and is the life force behind, in and through the physical body.

As a person becomes more conscious of their thoughts, feelings, desires, attitudes, emotions, beliefs, etc., they become more aware of the energy levels.

When you become more conscious of the energies you register and pick up on, you begin to have more free will. In other words, you have a choice whether or not to identify with any specific energy frequency.

The day you consciously choose not to identify with any thought, feeling, emotion or desire energy is the day you begin weaving the body of light.

The body of light is a third body, the spiritual body, what the ancient Egyptians called the sahu body. The body of light is created through the transmutation of negative energies attached to the energy body.

Many years ago I studied alchemy. The true alchemist was involved in the transmutation process. He transmuted the base metals (negative psychic energies) into gold (the light substance utilized in the forming of the body of light).

The alchemists, the philosophers, the masters, the masons, the Rosicrucians, the kabalists, the Sufis...spiritual teachers around the world on every continent since time immemorial have taught the mystery of weaving the body of light.

When I first came across this idea of a body of light (to me, then, it was only an idea), I contemplated, meditated and read everything I could find about the body of light. I used to ask myself, "Where is this light?", "How can I experience it?", "Can I see it?", "Can I feel it?". These questions and more occupied my thoughts day and night for months.

One day I got on a bus in Manhattan, sat down and looked around at the other passengers. A woman passenger sitting across the way had a hostile look on her face. When I glanced at her a torrent of negative energy poured out of her toward me. Apparently she did not want me, or anyone else for that matter, to see her negativity.

Anyway, just as I began feeling this wave of negativity impinging on my aura and then pulling and stabbing at my solar plexus energy center, I decided to see her negativity as light.

At that moment something quite remarkable happened. From that day forward my whole life changed.

As the flow of negative energies came across the bus aisle toward me it transformed/transmuted into light (positive/constructive energies). Actually, instead of feeling drained by the experience, which I would have been in the past, I got off the bus feeling energized.

What happened to me on a bus in Manhattan that day is the crux of how the body of light forms. Everytime you choose to sense-feel a negative energy within you/without you as light you literally create another strand of light woven into the body of light.

Eventually, as you get into the habit of transmuting negative energies into light, you form the body of light. Then, you consciously become a being of light functioning in a body of light.

The body of light is more subtle than the energy body. Its vibrational rate is much higher. You radiate a measure of light to everyone, everywhere you go. You transmute darkness, pain, suffering, sickness and disease wherever you go.

People feel better when they are around you. You energize their energy body. They feel the love within the light and know, on some level, that they are in The Presence.

You are a being of light,
Lost in the maze of night;
Open your sleepy eyes
The sun is about to rise.

Whatever you touch is light,
Awareness makes it bright;
Feel the fire transform
Cold flesh to soul warm.

All around you is light,
Stop, right now, alright;
See-feel-touch-know that all
Is light from cosmic big to atom small

Light Wave 99

Summary

1. Love permeates light presence.
2. Radiate light directing it to all who require more light.
3. The light regenerates.
4. Light transmutes memories of form, gravity, disease and death.
5. You are a light being in a dynamic light world.
6. Deep in the heart of every plant, animal and human cell is a foci of energy with estimated temperatures of from 3,000 - 6,000 degress F. These tiny suns are called "hot points" or "radiogens".
7. Say-feel-know each part of your body is light. Bring your attention to each part as you say, "this is light".
8. You do not have to wait until later to experience the light. You can experience it today, right now!
9. There are seven prerequisites that must be mastered before the light can shine in your life continuously.
10. They are: 1) a functionally trained mind, 2) purification of the psychic centers, 3) emotional control and calm, 4) physical repose, 5) measured speech, 6) creative use of energy and 7) living with purpose.
11. The negative energies emanating and vibrating from people and places, auras and atmospheres, build up destructive force-fields. When you feel your energy level dropping, it may be time to consciously connect with the light.

12. The light will protect and regenerate you, repulsing the negative emanations of destructive thought, feeling, desire, emotion, etc. At the same time, whatever psychic pollutants that have collected in your aura will be transmuted by the light into finer frequencies and wavelengths of energy.
13. By invoking the light you attract the light to you. The invoking process is simply asking with deep sincerity, gratitude and reverence that the frequencies of light protect, assist, purify and enlighten.
14. The day you consciously choose not to identify with any thought, feeling, emotion or desire energy is the day you begin weaving the body of light.
15. The body of light is a spiritual body, what the ancient Egyptians call the sahu body. The body of light is created through the transmutation of negative energies attached to the energy body.

About The Author

Greg Nielsen has been "treading the path" in this life since the 60's. Through a synchronistic series of events, he awakened to psychic and spiritual experiences.

Visions, dreams, vivid perceptions, chakra awakening, master teachers and the school of hard knocks have organically shaped his spiritual spiral.

He is the co-author of two international best-sellers, Pyramid Power and Pendulum Power. His second book on the pendulum, Beyond Pendulum Power, has been acknowledged as a classic in the field of dowsing and the pendulum.

Greg also practices and teaches astrology. He has written numerous astrology articles.

His life is dedicated to articulating and disseminating a science of living. His dream, and major life goal, is to see small groups of people dedicated to learning, practicing and teaching a science of living based on spiritual principles.

About the Artist (first edition)

Joanne Dose received her training in commercial and fine art at the Art Institute of Chicago and the University of Wisconsin at Madison.

An accomplished visionary artist, Joanne has designed the cover and illustrated the 1986,1988 and 1990 Celestial Influences Astrology Calendar, Pocket Astrologer and Celestial Guides.

A national following of private collectors display her higher self and light being portraits in their homes and offices.

A series of limited edition lithographs are in the works with a new age, visionary theme. Those interested in limited editions contact Joanne through Conscious Books.

Note

Greg Nielsen is available for talks, workshops, seminars, speaking engagements and book signings for your group, bookstore or organization. In addition, he is available for Pendulum Life Readings and Astrology Charts. Also, to find out when he is coming to your area write:

Greg Nielsen
Concious Books
316 California Ave., Suite 210
Reno, Nevada 89509
USA
or call: 800/322-9943
greg.nielsen@charter.net

www.ingramcontent.com/pod-product-compliance
Lightning Source LLC
Chambersburg PA
CBHW022017090426
42739CB00006BA/173